BREAKING

OUT

OF RELIGIOUS
CHRISTIANITY

BREAKING

OUT

OF RELIGIOUS
CHRISTIANITY

by

Reverend Duane Harlow

Destiny Image® Publishers, Inc.

P.O. Box 310
Shippensburg, PA 17257-0310

"Speaking to the Purposes of God for this Generation and for the Generations to Come."

ISBN 10: 0-7684-2383-X

ISBN 13: 978-0-7684-2383-9

This book and all other Destiny Image, Revival Press, MercyPlace, Fresh Bread, Destiny Image Fiction, and Treasure House books are available at Christian bookstores and distributors worldwide.

1 2 3 4 5 6 7 8 9 10 11 / 09 08 07 06

For a U.S. bookstore nearest you, call
1-800-722-6774.

For more information on foreign distributors, call
717-532-3040.

Or reach us on the Internet:
www.destinyimage.com

ENDORSEMENTS

This stimulating book can make a huge difference in your world, giving you the courage to launch into a deeper adventure with Jesus. Duane Harlow has an amazing gift to hear God's voice and sense what He is doing. As you read *Breaking Out of Religious Christianity*, you too will hear Father's voice more clearly as you journey into your unique destiny.

—Dr. Joseph Winger
Pastor on staff at Newlife
Colorado Springs, Colorado

Duane Harlow practices what he preaches. He is a man of extreme passion for Jesus and the Body of Christ. In *Breaking Out of Religious Christianity* he wonderfully touches God's heart for His people and His Church. The book will be a healing balm to anyone who is in love with Jesus and yet has become frustrated or disillusioned with the Church. It will challenge, encourage, and inspire each of us to truly become the 21st century Christians that Jesus has called us to be.

—Chris Jackson
Pastor, Springs Harvest Fellowship

The faith of Christianity in America is undergoing great change. Status quo is being challenged and mediocrity is no longer acceptable. In *Breaking Out of Religious Christianity*, Duane Harlow contributes to this facelift by asking overdue questions and offering insightful answers.

—Dutch Sheets
Dutch Sheets Ministries
Colorado Springs, Colorado

God is continually offering new wine of the Spirit, but He will only pour it out into new wineskins. What is the new wineskin for you? In this outstanding book, Duane Harlow clearly shows you how to move forward to receive the full destiny that God has for you!

—C. Peter Wagner
Chancellor
Wagner Leadership Institute

When something gets boring—it no longer satisfies! This is true in every sphere of life and ministry. Is there a cure for boring, predicable "churchianity"? Of course there is—it is vibrant, relevant, relational Christianity! Duane Harlow does us a great service by showing us the way of escape from the trap of "religiousity" back into the reality of a life-giving relationship with the Christ Jesus. Join Duane and other pioneers by blazing a trail into the church of the future—yes, a church without walls—a life where God is alive and well on planet earth and nothing is predictable!

—Dr. James W. Goll
Cofounder of Encounters Network
Author of *The Seer, The Lost Art of Practicing His Presence, Dream Language* and more!

DEDICATION

To all those who think that what you do for Jesus is more important than who you are in Jesus. There is so much more for you to do when you are a human being and not a human doing.

"...*They took note that these men had been with Jesus*" (Acts 4:13).

ACKNOWLEDGMENTS

I wish to thank and express my sincere appreciation to the following people who have helped shape my life:

Reverend Robert (Butch) Pluimer, my first pastor, teacher, and a friend.

Pastor John (Bud) Suitor, my friend, teacher, counselor. He gave me the opportunity to become.

Pastor John Wimber, the pastor who freed me to be who I am and to become all I could be.

Reverend Samuel Huddelson, who taught me how to love beyond my race and color. In fact, I think we worked on each other.

My wife Marlene, my friend and encourager, and the one who knows when I need a little more love than usual.

My Dad and Mother who remained sources of inspiration to me until their passing at the ages of 100 and 96 respectively.

TABLE OF CONTENTS

PREFACE

"Religious Christianity" is a stifling conviction of the mind and "Conservative Christianity" is a conviction of the heart—neither are a call from God. However, I believe that "Dynamic or Radical Christianity" is a conviction of the heart *and* a call from God!

Look at yourself and discover where you are in your development process as part of the Body of Christ. Ask yourself: Is there a fire burning in my heart for God? Is my relationship with the Living God lukewarm or am I living moment to moment for Jesus Christ? Remember that you cannot find the things that please God if you are not looking. Read His Word and discover or rediscover—then do it (see James 1:22).

There is a place in every church for people who are on fire for the Kingdom of God. If you feel as if your church is dead, then, as much as is possible, be part of the solution. Bring a fresh breath of life into it with your fire and not just with your words. The fire of God can come at any time, but it only stays when you are in a right relationship with Him.

My hope is that this book will help you understand what that means and how to have a dynamic, intimate, fire-breathing relationship with the Living God.

—Duane Harlow

CHAPTER 1

UNDERSTANDING

(Change Is Inevitable)

UNDERSTANDING may come late for some of us, but thank God, it comes and keeps on coming. The truth of the old adage that "change is inevitable" can be found throughout life; and as we look around we can see evidence that God, our unchanging God (see Mal. 3:6 and James 1:17), has created an ever-changing world. God, who never changes, created change. From the paths that the planets travel to the smallest grain of sand, all things change. God made the seasons to contrast with one another and beautiful flowers to bloom in the spring and to hide in the winter. The mighty granite mountains even change—though ever so slowly—as wind and rain etch their lasting marks on them.

Then, of course, there is you and I. We are in a constant flow of change—spirit, soul, and body. Changes in our physical bodies are by far the easiest of these to recognize: graying hair, sagging midriffs, wrinkles, and other reminders that we are in a process of change. Those of us who are in Christ Jesus are experiencing changes in a deeper way. We are being transformed, for our spirits, along with His Spirit, are being moved in a stream of life to become more like Him (see Rom. 6:4 and 2 Cor. 5:17). We are new creations; the old is gone, and the new is becoming!

A time of change has also come upon the Body of Christ. We have entered into a wonderful time when God, the Lord of all creation, desires to reveal more of Himself to us. I believe the ultimate transformation that He has in mind doesn't stop with the individual, but goes much further, into the Body of Christ, the Church, which He wants to revolutionize.

Picture God as a huge iceberg. From the water's surface, only about a third of the iceberg is visible; the rest remains hidden from view. Likewise, there is so much more of God to see and learn about, even to experience. (I believe that we, the Church, have been fixated only on that part of God that is visible and have been missing most of who He really is.) Now imagine an incredible heat blasting this frozen mountain. As the iceberg begins to melt, it deposits fresh water (His Spirit) into the surrounding water—now the two are becoming one. Likewise God is adding to us by revealing more of Himself to us, and as a result, we are continually changing into His image and likeness.

SPEAK TO ME

About two years ago on a summer Sunday morning, the Lord spoke a word into my heart that changed my life and became the impetus for this book.

I had just finished my shower, and my wife Marlene and I were listening to some worship music while getting ready for church.

I found myself caught up in the worship, when all of a sudden, I heard the words, "I hate Conservative Christianity" come out of my mouth. If I had false teeth, they would have shot across the room. My mind was racing. *Where did that thought come from?* Tears gushed down my face. With great force, I spoke it out to my wife. "What did you say?" she asked. As I repeated it for her the Lord began to give me understanding: "What do you think was conservative about My dying on the Cross? What do you think was conservative about the way My disciples lived and died?"

I was so shaken by those thoughts that I felt as if I had stuck my finger in a light socket. A few weeks later, loaded and cocked with this new revelation in my heart, I shared my experience with the congregation in a church where I was a guest speaker. "I hate conservative Christianity," I proclaimed. The place got very quiet. I'm not positive, but I think the color quickly left the pastor's face as he wondered where I was going and how he might repair the damage. As I explained my statement, I think he began to relax, and others moved to the edge of their chairs, eager to hear more.

"Conservative Christianity" is a modern term that was coined long after Jesus and His first disciples walked the earth. I will deal with what that term means to me in Chapter 2; but for now, please understand that whenever Conservative Christianity is used to explain someone's Christian belief system, it makes me see red. Likewise, Religious Christianity is as upsetting, for it limits the personal relationship Jesus desires to have with us.

Reflecting back to the Sunday morning when the Lord first spoke the phrase, "I hate conservative Christianity," to me, I am now more convinced than ever that this is the heart of God. How can I explain this? Here is a word that came in the same way as Revelation 2:15—God *hates* the doctrine of the Nicolaitans (not the Nicolaitans, but their doctrine) or in Proverbs 6 where God lists seven other things that He hates:

> There are six things which the Lord hates, Yes, seven which are an abomination to Him: [1.] Haughty eyes, [2.] A lying tongue, [3.] Hands that shed innocent blood, [4.] A heart that devises wicked plans, [5.] Feet that run rapidly to evil, [6.] A false witness who utters lies, [7.] And one who spreads strife among brothers (Proverbs 6:16-19 NASB).

Those who say that God is too loving to hate anything simply haven't read or have chosen not to believe the Bible. Yes! You are right. He does not hate people, but He *does* hate that which tries to destroy His Body, such as gossip, the things listed in Proverbs 6, divorce (see Malachi 2:16), and many other things.

A NEW REVELATION

Back to that Sunday morning. I felt despair and depression, and then anger. I was shown that a lie had been placed on the Church (by the authority that goes with the office of church leader) and we have swallowed this lie, hook, line, and sinker. It is not that authority is not part of the calling or office of leader; however it has become an all-consuming power trip for far too many, and we didn't even put up a good fight against it.

For many years, church leaders who impose their own views on their congregations, rather than encouraging members to search the Scriptures for themselves, have led us down this path of "religious piety, control, and manipulation" packaged with teachings that sound great but have what I call "worship of man." We have somehow learned to follow man (idol worship) and what he thinks, instead of following God and His Word. Just because a man is a great teacher does not mean that what he is teaching is correct. We must be discerning Christians. Blind faith in Christ is a great virtue, but blind faith in man is just blind.

I had a new revelation of what the "system" had stolen from the Church, the Body of Christ. First, let me explain what I mean when I say "system."

The Church today has gone through a great change from what the Bible describes as the Church of God. All the pastors, bishops, priests, and organizations that have ever existed have adjusted today's church. They have placed their own views and emphasis on certain Scriptures, often purporting only what they believe to be the correct interpretation or application, to the point where many people cannot agree with them. Even the long list of commentaries I have read do not totally agree with each other.

In their effort (which in most cases is honest and heartfelt) to bring understanding to the people of God, church leaders have chosen to manipulate the Scriptures to reflect what they think is the correct interpretation or application. This manipulation has led to what I call "churchianity" or "churchology." There are now so many views of what Christianity is supposed to look like that most Christians are confused as to what they truly believe.

Unity of understanding of the Scriptures in the Body of Christ no longer exists. It can't. We are so passionate about what we think we believe that we cannot let ourselves ponder what we don't understand. It might hurt someone's view of the narrow path that most of us have been taught to walk.

PRAYERFUL RECONSIDERATIONS

While I was pastor of Ramona Valley Christian Center in San Diego, California, I had a vision. We were meeting for prayer before the beginning of the evening service, as we often did, and we were in a circle on the platform worshiping when I saw a picture of a human spine. In the vision, the spine was being used as a bullwhip by some invisible hand, and as the bullwhip cracked, the top part of it broke off and flew away. I had the impression that it had to do with the cleansing of the temple as the Lord Jesus had done. However, it was not in the past; it represented what was to take place in the future. I was confused at the time because I knew that if this was representative of what was to take place in the Body of Christ, then why would the top of the spine be broken off? I knew that Jesus is the head and we are the body. I saw that it was not the head that was the point of the vision. It was that which was directly below the head—the leadership was going to be snapped off! What did that mean? Did this speak of the larger Body of Christ, or was it me? I knew this change was coming to the body and that it must include me as I was a *"senior pastor."*

We have seen much of this cleansing in the recent past. Nationally known leaders have fallen into sexual sin, divorce has run through the leadership of many churches, and there is more to come. God is not pleased with what we, as pastors and leaders, have done with His Church. Oh, for sure, He loves us and has forgiven us, but change must come, and it must come soon.

As Jesus cleansed the temple, He cried out that His Father's house was a house of prayer. Now we have again turned it back into a place of money changers. Something has gone terribly wrong. This change has been subtle, and our motives have not been all wrong, but we have to pump everyone we can for all the money we can, just to keep the machine rolling.

Here is a Word from the Lord that Marlene (my wife) received. She was at a healing service, and the Lord spoke to her, saying, "Prayer is the immune system for the Body." The immune system is the normal physical body system that functions to help cells communicate and fight off any disease that tries to infiltrate the body with infection. This system must be kept built up at all times so the body has a fighting force to keep it strong and healthy.

I see prayer as an interchange, a divine interchange between mankind and God. It is not meant to be a monologue—me talking with God, but rather a dialogue between the Creator and His children. God not only hears our prayers, but if we listen, He speaks life-changing truth to us that we can get no other way, and He speaks often.

While pastoring my first church things were great for the first few years. Then the Lord began to challenge me with words such as, "Duane, I want to know what you believe." Up until that time, I only taught others what I had been taught. I spoke like a parrot, repeating only what I heard others say. The realization that this was not pleasing to God really hurt because it was all I knew how to do—but it also changed my life and my ministry. God began to reveal Himself to me. I was full of questions that were not being answered by those who had trained me to pastor. To be fair, they couldn't answer the questions that were in my heart. Such questions were between God and me. For the first time in my ministry, He wanted me to develop my own understanding of what His Word was saying.

He was forcing me to cultivate my own views and beliefs. It was a great time of revelation and learning.

After five years, we had a congregation that loved us. We were bursting at the seams, and we were making plans to buy a larger church in the same neighborhood. In the midst of this seemingly successful ministry, my wife and I were dying. My children were headed in the wrong direction, and we were desperate to understand what was happening. Here we were; we had a successful church and we were loved, but things at home were spoiling. I was teaching the Word five times a week. My wife was laying her life down for the women. What was going on? We knew that if there was to be any hope for our family, we had to make big changes and make them quickly.

To the shock of the church, I resigned as pastor, and we moved back to Orange County, where we lived previously. Then after about a year of dying to our dreams, we found a church that believed God wanted to run things Himself. That, in itself, was enough to cause a great deal of thought in us. The view that had been modeled for us was that running things was the pastor's job and that the buck stopped with him. But where does the buck stop if God is the head of the church? With Him! What a great idea. I wonder who thought up that concept? I think that most pastors and leaders believe this (hopefully) but are too afraid to let go and see what God will do.

Now the question came to me: "What had we been doing all those years?"

We had learned that we were to *trust the Holy Spirit* and not just good teaching that we had heard along the way. What a revelation! Not that the teaching in itself was wrong, but faith was personal; it had to belong to me. Oh, the words had always been there, but truly learning to walk the truth hit me like a ton of bricks—we can be free to hear from God ourselves! It's not just the pastor that hears from God, but everyone who believes.

This truth came at me from two directions. One: I realized that I was not the real teacher—the Holy Spirit is. Two: people were going to hear from God in a unique, personal way— maybe different from the way I taught. For a pastor who always had to be in control, this truth was scary! We need to follow the Holy Spirit and not one man, no matter how nice he is or how well he teaches.

NOTHING BUT FEAR AND FACTS ARE HOLDING YOU BACK

I was so grieved with the understanding of what I had been doing all those years, (causing people to trust in me and my understanding of what God was doing and saying), that I called all the people from our previous church together. Marlene and I met with them and I repented for controlling what they were able to learn about God from me. After that I pointed them toward the Holy Spirit and told them that they should get their understanding of who God is and what He is doing from the Holy Spirit. Get it straight from the source, firsthand! I told them I had learned that God wanted to run His own Church. Imagine that! I am not saying that there isn't a place for the teaching pastor to practice his calling, but I do believe that he must give place to the Holy Spirit to say it to people the way He wants to. It is so exciting when people get it themselves. Lights go on, and they can't wait to share it with anyone who will listen. We (teachers) lead, and they follow.

All these events took place back in the late 1970s and early '80s and I have shared it all so you understand that even after I had been in the pastorate for more then 27 years, the Lord is continuing to stretch me and to teach and direct my life. Dying to our views is not fun or quick, but growing in the Lord is marvelous and rewarding. Don't be stuck! Get out of your boat and live! Do you think Peter was ever the same after he walked on water?

Be teachable. Be willing to learn new things from the Lord, for the Holy Spirit never stops teaching us about God. We will never be able to contain all that He is, but the more we know of Him, the more we will enjoy who He is and who we are in Christ.

What Is God Speaking to Me?

_____

_____

_____

_____

_____

_____

_____

_____

_____

_____

_____

_____

_____

_____

_____

_____

_____

_____

_____

_____

_____

_____

CHAPTER 2

I HATE "CONSERVATIVE" CHRISTIANITY

(What It Means to Me)

I understand that the word "conservative" may mean something different to almost everyone who hears it spoken. Webster's New World Dictionary defines conservative as: 1. To maintain; 2. Hostile to change; 3. To preserve; 4. Disposed to maintain existing institutions. The very word "conservative" has walls around it to keep it from becoming more. Attaching "conservative" to the church or as a prefix with Christianity has, by definition alone, hindered people from becoming true disciples of the living God, should they concede to its meaning. I believe that Christianity is supposed to be *dynamic*, an ongoing relationship like the revelation of Christ Jesus our Lord. Webster says something "*dynamic*" is a "physical force producing *motion*."

When I think about Jesus, the way He lived, what it must have been like for God the Son to allow Himself to be hung on the

Cross, I'm hit with this question: What was conservative about that? It was not only the way Jesus died on the Cross that was not conservative, but from His conception to His bodily resurrection, there was nothing conservative about the life of Jesus. The fact is, His life was radically different from anyone else's. Natural, but different!

And when I think about the disciples and the early Christians and how they lived and died, I wonder, what was conservative about that? For example, some were sawed in half, some were fed to the lions, some were dipped into tar and oil and then burned as lamps, and at least one was crucified upside down.

IN OTHER WORDS...

Synonyms for the words *radical* and *conservative* include: *Radical*—reformer, revolutionary, reformational, extreme. *Conservative*—antiquated person, preservative, unprogressive.

As I was shaving one morning, God asked me: "Tell Me, from which one of the examples that I left you to follow did you learn to be conservative?" Christianity was never intended to be conservative in nature. Conservative Christianity has created "Comfortable Christianity" and Religious Christianity. The Church has tamed Christianity by taming the full expression of the Holy Spirit and how He is allowed to function in our midst. Christianity was designed by God to be *radical* and *untamed* like the men Jesus chose to carry it to the ends of their earth. How far would Christianity, the message of Christ and our salvation, have gone if it were carried by nice, quiet, respectful men and women who had little or no understanding of how to fight, or how to war in the Spirit? Rejection would have stopped every one of those who were sent out.

> *From the days of John the Baptist until now, the kingdom of heaven has been forcefully advancing, and forceful men lay hold of it* (Matthew 11:12).

Comfortable Christianity creates buildings full of Christians who are no longer willing to take steps of faith—faith spelled r-i-s-k. The church in America is more willing to throw money at a problem than to throw themselves into the problem as part of the solution. We support television ministries that tell us of all the wonderful things they are doing for us. We support ministries that feed the poor rather than going out and helping out. We support those who take in the damaged people of this world, and yet we turn our backs on the homeless and unwed mothers. We are too busy with our lives to be what Paul told the Ephesians they (we) should be.

> *From him the whole body, joined and held together by every supporting ligament, grows and builds itself up in love, as each part does its work* (Ephesians 4:16).

We have come to the understanding that "our part" is centered on our money. I am not against para-church ministries, but the way I read the Word, it calls each one of us to be ministers and servants.

A radical thinker has started every powerful move of God. A peculiar person by-passed the establishment's narrow views and carried a gospel of grace and power, one that included all men, one that gave women the right and responsibility for their own relationship with Jesus, and one about a God who did not conform to the expectations of man. This God sends people out to a hurting and dying world.

How sad it is that so many Christians possess the ability to look past the spiritual and see only the physical. This is the opposite of the truth of God. God would rather have us look past the physical and see the spiritual. An example of this is when Jesus ministered in His hometown. The Bible says that He could not do many miracles there. The people were (and we are) in a battle with the facts, and the facts win out far too often.

How can we look back at the inheritance that has been left for us by the disciples and not be sick at heart and filled with grief for the state of the Church today? I do not mean the people who are the true Church—Jesus died for them, but He did not die for the "system."

Today's Church has been infected with a cancer that I call "the system," which controls people and quenches their appetites for more of God. This system, which has been entangled with conservative Christianity, was planted by the enemy to destroy the Church. Think about this! When Jesus left the earth and the Holy Spirit came, He came with fire and ignited the people of God with a white-hot fervor that caused them to go out and spread the Word of God throughout the known world. Every place where Christianity flourished, it broke out with fire and with signs and wonders.

This fire eventually cost the disciples their lives, yet they were dynamic in their testimony. They refused to be quieted. They were filled with a zeal that we still see today, especially in new believers. They believe; and then imitate what Jesus did in the

Bible. Jesus said to us, "*You, too, can do these things and even more.*" (See John 14:12 paraphrased.) New believers "*do these things*" until polluted by well-meaning but deceived brothers and sisters in Christ (who cave in to peer pressure). They have yet to be tainted by those who love the system and its conservative views. You know, those who want to mold them and make them into their *own image* of what is acceptable in their *own view* of the perfect church.

ALL THINGS FAMILIAR

I think the reason (or at least one of the reasons) for the dispersal of the first church (the great persecution) from Jerusalem is that the church was becoming conservative—ingrown. God, using the same ways He used in the past, caused an outside source (outside of the Body of Christ) to come against His people who were not carrying out the Great Commission. The message, the Good News of Jesus Christ, needed to be dispersed. But for many reasons—including fear of reprisals, the unknown, risk taking and leaving behind all things familiar—they were circling the wagons and not moving on. These are, of course, many of the same reasons that we don't go out and preach the Good News to everyone we meet.

Here is a typical example from my own life that illustrates how the system will control us if we allow it. This may sound small and even silly, but for me at the time, it was big.

There is a couple who played a large part in the making of Duane, the disciple. These two people frustrated me to no end—although I love them and will always see them as teachers who helped me get off my religious high horse. Everyone knows that when someone gets saved, that that person is "born again." Right? Well, not with this lady. She just wouldn't say the "right" words! The correct way was to say "born again." To her, though, it was "twice born." I mean, after all, don't you know that there is a right way and a wrong way to say things?

When I was in the Navy there was a saying, "There is the right way, the wrong way, and the Navy way." Well, in order for anything to be correct, it had to be my way or the way I had been taught. One might think that those who are being born again are perfect. Yes, I know that when we come into the Kingdom of God, we are brand new creatures in Christ. But have you noticed that it takes some time for our old habits to get the message? By the way, I changed and she didn't. But at the time, I wanted everything in black and white.

When I was saved, these were the type of things that were being said or modeled by the older saints, who I am sure wanted the best for me and hoped that they might save me from the mistakes that they had made. "You must not drink, smoke, cuss, dress like an individual, or wear your hair long (men)." And in many churches, you still cannot think for yourself. It was communicated to me that it was very dangerous to have your own opinions about what the Bible says. With this type of modeling, it's not long before new believers begin to lose the zeal they showed by acting on the Word of God alone, without doubt. People take new believers, wash them in their church doctrines, and believers come out acceptable, lukewarm, and "conservative."

TURN UP THE HEAT

Lukewarm is defined as: moderately warm; tepid; indifferent.

I remember a sad experience in my early Christian life when I waited two weeks for an appointment with the pastor of a very large church in Orange County where Marlene and I had been baptized. When I arrived I had to wait, so I shared some of my excitement with the pastor's secretary. She made a remark that hurt me so much that after 30 years, I still remember it. She said, "Just wait awhile, and all that excitement will leave." Now that's what I call pollution! Why would anyone want to dampen the enthusiasm and zeal of a new believer? I don't believe that this is what she really wanted, but that is what it did.

In August 1999, Marlene and I personally received a prophecy from a friend that said, "There is a 'Cancer of Compromise' in the Body of Christ."

Oh, yes! This word has helped me understand what has been slowly and silently eating away at the Body of Christ. *Compromise, comfortable Christianity, conservatism.* These are straight from the pit of hell. From satan himself!

In my view, this comes very close to Revelation 3:16: "*So, because you are lukewarm—neither hot nor cold—I am about to spit you out of my mouth.*"

It could also be related to the ten virgins of Matthew 25:10-12: "*But while they were on their way to buy the oil, the bridegroom arrived. The virgins who were ready went in with him to the wedding banquet. And the door was shut. Later the others also came. 'Sir! Sir!' they said. 'Open the door for us!' But he replied, 'I tell you the truth, I don't know you.'*"

John 16:1-3 says, "*All this I have told you so that you will not go astray. They will put you out of the synagogue; in fact, a time is coming when anyone who kills you will think he is offering a service to God. They will do such things because they have not known the Father or me.*"

These were the biblical scholars of their day. No one knew more about God than they did. They were it! If you wanted to know something about God you would ask them. Yet Jesus tells us that, *"They did not know the Father or me."* Knowing about God is never enough! As you read on you may hear this again and again, and I will not apologize—it's too important. *Knowing about God* is only part of the equation.

SO MUCH HAS BEEN STOLEN FROM US

Who we are, who we really are in Christ, has been stolen from us, even to the point that when we get around people who are beginning to understand their real identity, the one given to us by the death of Jesus, the one attained by those willing to die daily on their own cross, we judge them and brand them as heretics. Why? They scare us; they are outside of our control and our belief system.

Who are we? What is the Cross, His death, and His resurrection all about? What is the result? Just people who believe in Jesus? I don't think so. That would fall very short of what new life in Christ is truly all about. After all, satan believes in Jesus—I don't want to be numbered with him. Well, then what? Sons! Daughters! You mean those who are adopted into the Body of Christ? Yes, but that is only part of it. There is so much more!

Word: *We serve an absolutely incredible God.*

I Am the beat of life. As music would not have an order without the beat, I Am the beat of life. I hold all things together by my Word. It is I who speak life to your soul to cause birth. I speak life to your spirit so you can commune with My Spirit. I alone adorn the world with light, and I give life to all living things. You exist because I spoke. You live because I gave you breath. I alone Am God!

What Is God Speaking to Me?

_____

_____

_____

_____

_____

_____

_____

_____

_____

_____

_____

_____

_____

_____

_____

_____

_____

_____

_____

_____

_____

_____

_____

_____

CHAPTER 3

HE SPEAKS, BUT AM I LISTENING?

(God's DNA In Us)

I had a vision as I was speaking with some friends. I saw a room filled with lambs from wall to wall. I heard a voice say, "The lost sheep of Israel." I began to argue with the voice and said, "But these are saved; they're in the Church," He then said, "But they don't have a clue!"

I knew He meant that they had no understanding of who they are in Christ or who He really is. This hurt deep in my heart. I also knew that God was calling me to go back into the "system" so I can help those in the Church *"grow to know"* who God has made them to be and who Jesus really is. I say *back in* because for some time, I have been pulling away from the "system of the Church." Again let me say that I don't mean the *people* who are the Church.

The system has destroyed the Church and caused it to be weak, full of apathy, anemic, and in desperate need of a blood transfusion. Blood is life to the body, and the Body of Christ needs a fresh transfusion from Jesus so the Church can once again be a strong, dynamic source of life.

The Bible says in First John 3:9 that anyone born of God has the "*seed of God*" in him or her. What do you suppose this means? It means absolutely everything! The word "seed" is the word *sperma*, which is Greek for the word *sperm*. Do you see it? We have the DNA (Deoxyribonucleic Acid) of God in us! What does this really mean? It's all about the reproduction of His life in us! Why?

Genesis 1:26-27 says "*In our image...[I] created them.*" We serve a God of passion. What do I mean when I say that God is a God of passion? First, let us look at a creation verse: Genesis 2:7 "*Then God formed the man from the dust of the ground and breathed into his nostrils the breath of life.*" The imagery is that of a potter and his clay. If you had the task of creating an image of yourself, what kind of effort would you put forth to make it right? God first took dirt, clay, dust of the ground. This is, by definition the picture of a potter, some clay, and a wheel. Think about it. God, as a Master Potter or Master Craftsman, is carving or shaping an image of Himself. Do you think He would want it to come out perfectly? If it were you, you would covet what you made. I believe that this is the passion that God has when He creates us. He covets what He makes. We are created by the hands of God the Potter. This is one of the most intimate tasks that anyone can perform. First you must be skilled and tender, always keeping the clay moist and pliable, and all of the time having a picture in mind of the end product. Created by touch, for touch. Created with care, for care. Created out of love, for love.

Now think about the breath that He breathed into Adam. The Bible narrows it down to the nostrils. I think it was mouth to mouth. The better translation of the word breathed is "puffed." You don't puff something from across the galactic space of the universe. You get up close. I believe it began with a kiss. God made us into creatures that would respond to touch and passion, and that is what He used to create us.

Jesus says this in John 17:21-23:

> *That all of them may be one, Father, just as you are in me and I am in you. May they also be in us so that the world may believe that you have sent me. I have given them the glory that you gave me, that they may be one as we are one: I in them and you in me. May they be brought to complete unity to let the world know that you sent me and have loved them even as you have loved me.*

God has planted His seed in us so we can be changed into His likeness. He doesn't call us sons and daughters just because He adopted us—he calls us family because He put His life in us. We truly have been born again. Brand-new babes. Not just taped on, but grafted in!

Once a branch has been grafted into a tree, everything changes; the DNA of the tree becomes infused with the DNA of the branch. It's new! It's no longer the branch and it's not just the tree. The two have become a new *one*. The fruit will not be the same as the branch or the tree, but will share the strongest parts of each.

This is what God has done with us. We have been infused with the DNA of the living God (Jesus), and we are no longer who we were. We are new! We are not Jesus, even though we now have His DNA flowing through us, but the longer we are connected to Jesus, the more we resemble Him—as *new creations*. Our fruit will be blessed with God in us, but we still have the individual flavor of who He made us to be from the beginning. What a deal! He forms us by hand for a particular purpose and then puts His life in us to accomplish that work.

I don't know about you, but I am truly blessed to know that the One True God, the God of all creation, is dwelling in me and has given me the right to dwell in Him.

Now, add this to the understanding of being adopted. Doesn't it bring so much more to the table? There is no place here for confusion. *We are family*. When Jesus calls us His brothers and sisters, it now has so much more meaning, not just believers in Christ but truly family.

Jeremiah 33:3 tells me that I can call on the Father and that He will reveal more truths that I, in my flesh, cannot search out. I'm not sure that "can" is the right word, because it looks like a statement not a request. In calling on the Father, I have been receiving more and more revelation that is leading me to acknowledge things that I have previously just speculated about. Jesus not only came as our Savior and Lord, but He came so we could see in real time what we are supposed to look like. He is our real life model! We are (have been) predestined to be conformed into His image and likeness. The word in Aramaic is *Icon*.

We, too, are children of God and joint heirs with Jesus. Paul says in the Book of Colossians that Jesus is the Icon (image, likeness, exact representation) of God and Jesus says that we are the Icon (same word) of Him (see Heb. 2:5-8). Psalm 8 says that man was made just a little lower than the angels. I believe that it says that man was made, created just a little lower than God (Elohim). If we are the Icon of Jesus and He is the Icon of the Father, this means that He made us as close to Himself as possible except He put us in a body, then sent our pattern, Jesus, God in the flesh, God the Son, to show us what we were created for.

HEARING THE VOICE OF GOD

It has been suggested by a pastor friend of mine who read this manuscript for me that the ability of Marlene and me to hear from the Lord might be as important as anything I have written in this book. My first impression was to question why. I guess we were very blessed to have the teacher we had many years ago when we first entered the Kingdom of God. One of the first things we were taught after crossing the border into the Kingdom was that God is never quiet. He loves to talk to His kids like any other father. I understand that there are many Christians who believe that the Bible is the only source of communication with God. I believe that although this source is vital to our relationship with the Lord, it is not the only source. We were taught that He loves to talk with us and that He is seldom silent. We have grown up in Christ believing that this is the *normal* and *natural* expectation that Christians should have. Possibly one of the reasons we do hear from the Lord is that we ask and expect for this communication to take place.

Believing that God wants to talk to me is as basic in my belief system as salvation, or healing, the virgin birth, and Jesus being God the Son. It goes along with His passion for His creation. Can you imagine loving someone so intensely and not wanting to talk with them? I can't!

One of my regular prayers is *"Call to me and I will answer you and tell you great and unsearchable things you do not know"* (Jer. 33:3). It just knocks me out to think that the God of all creation, my God, wants to tell me His secrets. Another of my regular prayers is *"Ask and it will be given to you; seek and you will find; knock and the door will be opened to you. For everyone who asks receives; he who seeks finds; and to him who knocks, the door will be opened"* (Matt. 7:7-8). As I have said, "When we pray, we expect an answer."

When we ask for wisdom and revelation, we expect wisdom and revelation. I suppose that understanding our relationship helps—it is not His desire to withhold any good thing from us (see Ps. 84:11). *"Seek and you shall find"* seems pretty straightforward to me. Our God is not out to trick us or lead us down a wrong or silent path.

If I can impart any advice in this area, it is this: Listen for His voice and get started right now. It takes some time to learn to trust what you are hearing and to know the difference between your hopes and what is truly from God. I am very secure in the knowledge that you will discover how eager He is to talk to you.

The Bible gives us some insight into the question of whether or not God speaks. In Hebrews 12:25: *"See to it that you do not refuse Him who speaks."* John's gospel relates Jesus' words that He only says what He hears the Father saying (John 12:49-50).

This is not to say that what I hear is what I ask or that the communication is in response to a direct question. I pray, asking or seeking, and He speaks what He wants, sometimes hours or days later and sometimes right away. Also, the shower is not the only place where I hear from Him although it has been a good place. Generally, I hear from God when my mind is peaceful, not stressed, and not demanding an answer. I never want to forget that no matter who I am in terms of my relationship with Him, or how important the message is that He has given me to share, He is God and I am not.

These scriptures, although not specific, say that God makes His will known: Deuteronomy 4:29,35-36; Jeremiah 29:12-13; Matthew 13:11; and Matthew 11:25. And there is the entire work we know as the Bible, or the Word of God. By itself, it gives everyone the understanding that God wants to communicate with us.

As an important point to consider, I do not believe that God speaks anything doctrinally that is outside the counsel of Scripture.

Word: As I looked at the communion table after we had shared it, and as I viewed what was left (the bread and juice), I felt as if the Holy Spirit was saying, "Don't let My Body or My Blood become stale now. You have enjoyed fellowship and intimacy with Me this morning; you have talked to Me and worshiped Me. You have eaten and tasted Me and found Me good. Now don't put this aside, what you have experienced this morning, until the next first Sunday of the month. I want your heart every day. I love the fellowship and the intimacy I had with you today, and I want to enjoy this all the time."

What Is God Speaking to Me?

_____

_____

CHAPTER 4

PICTURE THIS!

(Mary)

ONE day as I was getting ready for work, the Lord gave me a picture. He showed me the time when the Angel of the Lord came to Mary and told her that she was going to give birth to Jesus, the Christ.

WHAT A PICTURE!

The angel represents the evangelist who first came to share the good news with you. *"Greetings, you who are highly favored. The Lord is with you!"* (See Luke 1:28.) Now it may have come differently to you, but sometime in this conversation, the evangelist told you that Jesus loves you and that you are very special in His sight. Just think about that. You are highly favored with the Lord. When the Lord calls on your life (when someone shares the Gospel with you) no matter how rotten or good your life has been, you are highly favored with God. Why? Because He created you, made you, called you, and set you aside for something special called salvation, and He is now offering it to you without charge. The angel may not look like, act like, or smell like one of the Lord's angels, but that is what he or she represents. This evangelist may be just a friend or relative, but in this case the angel has been sent by God Himself to help bring you into His Kingdom.

I am reminded of the story of one of the angels that God used to help in the call of John and Carol Wimber. As I recall the story, it was Dick and Lynn Hines (he was the drummer on the worship team while Marlene and I were at the Vineyard in Anaheim, California). Dick and Lynn had just been saved and wanted their friends, John and Carol, to share in this experience. They arranged to visit with John and Carol, and on this cold night, they stopped and bought a fifth of something, thinking that it would warm up everyone. They were brand-new Christians, and the Lord had not yet showed them that there may be a better way.

While enroute they began to indulge themselves (remember it was a cold night), and by the time they arrived, they were drunk (this story can be found in John Wimber's video entitled, "I'm a Fool For Christ. Whose Fool Are You"). John Wimber told this story many times during the years we attended the Vineyard church. Of course, the end of the story is that Dick and Lynn were used by God for John and Carol. Step by step, God leads us to Him. Dick and Lynn did not lead John to salvation, but they were used by God to get him to the place were he could hear that message.

You may wonder how this incident could have been of God. Do you remember John the Baptist? He was totally different in his approach. He cursed and cussed out the religious leaders of his day. Or maybe you will remember the reluctant evangelist named Jonah! He had the nerve to tell God "no" when God told him to go spread His Word. When Jonah finally arrived at the place of his calling, he had to be a sight. A Christian comedian's description of the story of Jonah and the whale: Jonah was bleached out from stomach acid inside the whale, soaked with vomit and seaweed, and went through the city of Nineveh, prophesying for God. Oh, what a sight that must have been!

You cannot deny that these evangelists were all very different, and yet they were all very effective.

YOUR ANGEL

What was your angel like? Mine was more conventional—my sister Dawn and her husband Jay Hoyal. But what they did was not the norm. They went way over the line to bring me into the Kingdom of God, albeit I was kicking and screaming all the way and leaving skid marks on the floor as I entered.

I may or may not have already been saved, depending on your doctrine, but I know that what I call conversion had not taken place. (To me this means that I was not in any way serving anyone but myself and certainly not Jesus.) Dawn and Jay took in my two children to live with them and their five children so that I could get my life straightened out. They kept my children with them for eight months while I tried to let Jesus make life worth living again. God had much work to do in Marlene and I, and He did it in short order.

Of course, this process still goes on today, 30+ years later. Remember, angels (those people sent by God to you) may have human skin and even be people you know well. Don't miss it! I am not saying that God's angels are human or that your human friends or family are real angels, but please hear only that God can and will use anything or anybody to do His work for Him. In many parts of the world today God is showing Himself to people and they are being saved.

Don't be like the religious people of Jesus' day who thought they were wired in—in the end they missed it.

Ok, now let's consider Mary. "I have the most wonderful gift for you. It's the greatest gift that anyone could ever receive. It cost more than any gift ever given, and it will cost you a great deal of pain and misunderstanding in your future." I believe that Mary represents what the Church of God is supposed to be: discipler, trainer, encourager. But something had to happen first. Mary had to be open to the Holy Spirit and what He wanted to do through her. Then she had to receive the Word of God ("*Be it unto me according to your word*") and become the vessel that housed the womb, that held the Son of God.

As I was praying one morning on the way to work, I had an impression about the conception of Jesus. What I felt was that Jesus was to be a mixture of God and man, a mixture of Mary's genes and those of God. I am not a theologian and I may be missing something, but isn't that what God did in us when He put His seed in us? *I am a mixture of man and God.* Why then, when I hold up the life of Jesus alongside of mine is there such disparity? I assume that the gene I receive or the DNA of God has not changed or been polluted, so I feel that I must look for the differences that exist between Mary and those who gave birth to me. I think we can find a key here for future generations.

The main difference I can easily see is that Mary was not one given to satisfying self. She was a woman (a very young woman) who was in awe of God and was culturally protected from much of what my parents experienced in their lives. Although my mother was a Christian, I would have to admit that she had lived a life, previous to having her children, that was not devoted to the things of God. As with most of us who are alive today, our human heritage has gone through quite a bit of pollution. And even after the seed of God has been implanted in us we must go through a great deal of restoration.

GODLY HERITAGE

The value of this understanding, I believe, would be for our children and heirs. If we can pass on more of the heritage of Mary (lives devoted to God), our heirs will be better off. This is not my feeble attempt to shift blame for my own lack of godliness, nor do I fix any blame nor do I wish to, but what I would like is that we might all get an understanding of just how important it can be for us to pass on a heritage with as much of God in it as possible. We do have an opportunity to help those with our same genetic code who will follow us in our quest for a life of intimacy with our God and a heritage we do not have to be ashamed to pass on.

Then the Bible says that the Holy Spirit overshadowed Mary. God was infusing His DNA with hers. The "rachaph" of God (the overshadowing) was taking place as He moved across her.

With love and protection, nourishment and guidance, Mary released Jesus (and God releases us) to become all He was birthed to be. Mary did not raise Jesus to become an expression of her, but she allowed God to have His way with Jesus. So Jesus was groomed by the Holy Spirit and by his earthly father and mother.

See with me the difference between Mary and Zechariah, the father of John the Baptist. When the angel of God came to Zechariah he wanted to know how it would be possible, and the angel had to quiet Zechariah so it could be done. Zechariah was full of unbelief and doubt so the Angel of the Lord shut Zechariah's mouth so that he could not speak his unbelief. Two examples for us to think about.

There is also the crib or manger. We believe it was just a feed trough, but what it represents is a secure environment. How important is it to protect that which is birthed of God. The Church is supposed to be a safe place to grow and protect babies from an enemy who wants to destroy everything of God.

God has given us this perfect gift—the seed of life in us—for us to culture and grow and develop so that He can be reproduced throughout the earth.

What Is God Speaking to Me?

_____

_____

_____

_____

_____

_____

_____

_____

_____

_____

_____

_____

_____

_____

_____

_____

_____

_____

_____

_____

_____

CHAPTER 5

A TRIAL

(Circumstances of Life)

I am currently faced with a very difficult set of circumstances in my life. In December 2000 my mother (age 91) had a stroke that has left her with a very confused mind. She doesn't know who her children are much of the time. On top of that, my stepfather, who has always taken care of her, fell and broke his hip and has also had a stroke. At the time of this writing he is 99 and very frail. Even if he recovers, he will not be able to take care of my mother anymore, for they both need 24-hour care.

Although this is a very difficult time for all of us, it is not the problem. The real problem is that even though they have a combined Christianity of more than 160 years, they still don't get it! Instead of feeling God's loving embrace through this time, they are convinced that God is getting even with them for something or some things they did in the past. They don't understand the mystery of the Church and the kind of love the Lord has for them or the extent of His forgiveness. The "system" has successfully blocked their learning curve by teaching them just one perspective, that of their denomination or pastor; and by not seeing the larger Kingdom of God they have lost hope. The system (structure) of their church has kept them worshiping a very controlling, demanding God, and, in my view, it has failed them. "My" God forgives us as far as the East is from the West.

If what they believe is true, then God is a liar, and we are all in big trouble. Our future is in doubt and we are all doomed to a life of guilt, fear, and despair. If you believe the Word of God, then you recognize how forgiving and loving our Lord God is. Even so, my mother and father both believe in Jesus and His Word, but they, along with many of the Christians in the Body of Christ that I have encountered in my life, believe that God is vengeful. They believe that He is waiting for a chance to get even with them for their sins. Understand this. His vengeance is reserved for His enemies, and that is not you or me if we are indeed His children.

This kind of truth makes religious Christians angry. They don't want anything to change their view of God. Change would cause them to become very insecure. They have built up the walls, structure, the *system*, in order to keep them safe from the world outside. Guilt is a major part of this system. Guilt has been used very effectively in sermons to get people to act the way their pastor thinks they should. In the past I have put such trips on God's people, all in the name of training them up.

CHRISTIAN WORKS VS. CHRISTIANS WHO WORK

Many people have never been freed from the understanding that they have to do something (works) to have a relationship with God. I think they view a relationship with God with the same perspective that they view relationships between people here on earth. Although this is close, it has a wrong base. They are confused between Christian works and Christians who work.

We don't work to have relationship with the Lord; we follow His lead (as in dancing) so we don't get our toes stepped on. No, don't think that way. Jesus does not step on our toes, but He will and does correct us and direct us. Even before we were born, He longed to have a relationship with us. All we have to do is yield to His direction. It's called being conformed to His image and likeness. It is a work of His Spirit. Let's go back to the original plan, before we *chose* to try to be like Him by eating from the tree of knowledge (see Genesis 2:9; 3:5).

I am not saying that my mother or father are not *saved* from eternal hell or that they will not be going to Heaven, but what about the whole purpose of being saved while still alive on earth? We are to represent Jesus and His Kingdom here and now. How can we accomplish this if we do not understand Sonship? If we don't realize who we are, then how can we truly represent our Heavenly Father?

The Word of God says that we are to "*put on the new* (Christ and His ways) *and put off the old*." (See Ephesians 4:17-32.) We must allow the process to go on, dying to self and living unto Him. It's all about Him; not all about us. He made us for "His" pleasure.

Then who is He? Who is this man who speaks to the wind and calms the seas? He is the designer of the wind and the sea! He speaks to the sick and they are healed. Why? He is also the designer of those who became sick.

Did you know that if we will allow it (by quieting ourselves), He will speak into our lives, and we, too, will be changed? Then it's up to us to follow (obey) the direction of His voice. He even wants to tell us where to go and what He wants to do through us. Remember that Jesus only did what He saw the Father doing and He only said what He heard the Father saying. Isn't He our example, and isn't that real relationship? Jesus wasn't following some stranger's voice while He was living here on earth. He wasn't letting some mere acquaintance tell Him what to do or where to go or who to heal. No! He had relationship with the Father, the Creator, the Designer!

Paul and Peter say it best in Second Corinthians and Second Peter: *"The weapons we fight with are not the weapons of the world. On the contrary, they have divine power to demolish strongholds"* (2 Cor. 10:4). These weapons have been given to us, in Jesus, and they are ours to use. The divine power is in us. It's a part of who we now are as His children. *"Through these he has given us his very great and precious promises, so that through them you may participate in the* **divine nature** *and escape the corruption in the world caused by evil desires"* (2 Peter 1:4 emphasis added). We have the very nature, the *divine nature of God* along with the *divine power of God*, growing and developing His seed planted in us to the point that we can and will do "greater things."

I am not saying that we are divine, but God has done everything to cause us to function as Christ did, and to be a Christ (Savior type) to the world. This is impossible for man unless we understand what Jesus really did for us.

When Jesus came to us, He was both God and man, but I believe that He only functioned here as man. I realize that some of you may disagree with this, but listen to my reasoning. If He had come as God, then we would have no hope to be able to accurately represent Him in any realistic way. Yet as Jesus had the divine in Him (I use this term only for illustrative purposes, for we know that He is divine), we also have the divine in us. He was our model, so it only stands to reason that we must be able to be like Him if we are to do the things He has sent us out to do, and then even greater things than He did.

What was Jesus' favorite name for Himself? Son of Man! (See Matt. 26:64; Mark 9:12; Luke 6:5; John 6:53.) Why? So you and I could find the common ground with Him in our humanity. He wants us to see Him as one of us. An illustration: Say you went out to buy a new car, and you picked out the very best one money could buy—you got every whistle and bell, every extra goody available by paying a high price for it. Before leaving the dealership, you asked the body shop mechanics to remove the driver's door. If you walk out of the dealership with only that one door, how much enjoyment and how effective would your vehicle be?

I believe that this is what most Christians have done. They get only a small piece of what they committed to, and then they wonder why they don't have joy or the power that they hoped salvation would bring; and yea, where's the "stuff"? What's the stuff? It's what all Christians are supposed to be doing—healing the sick, raising the dead, casting out demons. You know, all the bells and whistles stuff. Mark 16 stuff!

Not only do the verses in Romans 8:14-17 say that God recognizes us as His children, but it also says that He has given us all the same inheritance that Jesus has—"*co-heirs with Christ and Sons of God, Children of God.*" When I first read this many years ago, it was good news. Wow, we have been made children of God, and we have become joint heirs with Christ. To be truthful, I am just beginning to understand what this means. Sonship is so powerful, if only we can grasp the understanding of it (see Gal. 4:4-7). We have received full rights as sons and daughters and can call to our Daddy anytime we want to. We are heirs, family. This is so important, for we are sent out in the same way as Jesus was, to do the same works that He did with the same authority that He had. This was given to us by the same Father, God! How can we *consider ourselves less* than what He says we are? First John 3:2 relates to Genesis 3:22 and what we can expect at the endtime. We are joint heirs with Christ. We have been given life, in God, by God, for God's purpose. We are a new creation, one that has *never* existed before.

FROM GOD'S WORD

The following scriptures will communicate to your spirit.

"A farmer went out to sow his seed. As he was scattering the seed, some fell along the path; it was trampled on, and the birds of the air ate it up" (Luke 8:5). The parable of the sower—the Father is the gardener. He has spied out and prepared the land (you and me) where He wants to plant His seed.

"For we are God's workmanship, created in Christ Jesus to do good works, which God prepared in advance for us to do" (Eph. 2:10). We are God's "Work of Art" prepared in advance, hand-formed for His purpose.

"Instead, speaking the truth in love, we will in all things grow up into Him who is the Head, that is, Christ. From Him the whole body, joined

and held together by every supporting ligament, grows and builds itself up in love, as each part does its work. So I tell you this, and insist on it in the Lord, that you must no longer live as the Gentiles do, in the futility of their thinking" (Eph. 4:15-17). Here we see the seed grow and develop, and we see that it is part of a large crop.

"You were taught, with regard to your former way of life, to put off your old self, which is being corrupted by its deceitful desires; to be made new in the attitude of your minds; and to put on the new self, created to be like God in true righteousness and holiness" (Eph. 4:22-24). New life created to be like God in true righteousness and holiness. Truth in love, we will in all things grow up into Him.

"Be imitators of God, therefore, as dearly loved children" (Eph. 5:1). How could this be possible if we did not have God's blood in us? He gave us of Himself so that we could be imitators of God as dearly loved children. He loves His kids and gave us all we need to carry on His work.

"Our fathers disciplined us for a little while as they thought best; but God disciplines us for our good, that we may share in His holiness" (Heb. 12:10). He, as our Father, disciplines us for our good that we may share in His holiness. We are holy because He is holy, and He has imparted that Holiness to us. Growing in this holiness should be one of our goals.

"For those God foreknew He also predestined to be conformed to the likeness of His Son, that He might be the firstborn among many brothers" (Rom. 8:29). We have been predestined to be conformed to the likeness of His Son. Are you changing? Are you allowing the blood of Jesus to flow through your veins and bring about that transformation?

"With the tongue we praise our Lord and Father, and with it we curse men, who have been made in God's likeness" (James 3:9). Man is made in God's likeness. What a great gift.

"Therefore, if anyone is in Christ, he is a new creation; the old has gone, the new has come!" (2 Cor. 5:17). We are *"brand new creations"* not something remade, but brand new!

"A man ought not to cover his head, since he is the image and glory of God; but the woman is the glory of man." (1 Cor. 11:7). We are the image and glory of God.

These scriptures will *come alive* to you now.

"Not so with you. Instead, whoever wants to become great among you must be your servant, and whoever wants to be first must be your slave— just as the Son of Man did not come to be served, but to serve, and to give his life as a ransom for many." (Matt. 20:26-28). The King James Version uses the word "minister," instead of "serve." This says that Jesus was sent by the Father and came as a minister or servant and that we are sent in the same way.

"As You sent me into the world, I have sent them into the world" (John 17:18). Jesus said to the Father, "As You sent me into the world, I have sent them." The same way!

"Again Jesus said, 'Peace be with you! As the Father has sent me, I am sending you.'" (John 20:21). As the Father has sent me, "I am" sending you. Again it has the meaning of *in the same way*.

"Therefore go and make disciples of all nations, baptizing them in the name of the Father and of the Son and of the Holy Spirit" (Matt. 28:19). The Great Commission says to "Go in My Name." We have been commissioned by the Living God to do this work. The *key*: we are *sent* in the *same way* as Jesus was sent.

Ask yourself this. Why would we be sent in the same way, to do the same work as Christ and even greater works than He did, without having been given *the same authority and the same power and the same ability to accomplish this work*? I personally don't see how this would be even remotely possible!

I pray things are becoming clear to you as I expose the dangers of "Religious Christianity."

JUST THOUGHTS

God takes all I have done, all I have learned, and all that I have been taught to build my understanding of who He is and who I am. Experience on experience, teaching on teaching, and precepts on precepts. If we give it all to Him, He will use it, to teach and lead us into the understanding of what true godliness is all about.

Where I go, Lord, your mercy goes, along with your healing, your power, your love, your grace, all of You. It's not to conquer land but to subdue the enemies in the lives of your creation.

What Is God Speaking to Me?

_____

_____

_____

CHAPTER 6

IT'S NEVER ENOUGH?
GET JESUS!

THE fire of God is meant to consume us, so don't pray for the fire unless you are ready to give up "self." Rather pray for the water. The River of God is fun and filled with wonderful relationship and intimacy with Him, but the fire of God will burn up the flesh. Our flesh is as the fat offering to God, and the fire is meant to completely consume it. It's an offering of sacrifice to Him when we allow Him to send the fire and burn up that which does not bring glory to Him. However, He is God and is able to pour water on those who need water, and fire on those who are ready to give up all their rights and live only for Him.

As in the days of Noah, when water covered all the earth and washed away all the flesh, so now the River of God has come to cover all humanity. The first flood came to destroy flesh; now the River of Life has come to refill us and bring new life to us. The water must come first and then the fire, for our God is a consuming fire, and when He is revealed in us, He consumes us and burns away all that ugly fat. In a way, I'm like the younger generation (I am 60+) because I'm not satisfied with the status quo. I don't think it really matters which "younger generation" as it seems to pass from one to another. I know I want more, and I will always want more. "Got enough?" "Got enough yet?" I've tried it all, and I want more.

A LITTLE BIT OF JESUS IS LIKE A LITTLE BIT OF FOOD

A little bit of Jesus is not enough, nor is a little bit of love. Like a love letter written to a far-away loved one, a little bit of love may bring comfort for a short time, but later it causes a deep pain in the pit of your stomach. You yearn more and more until that time when you can once again hold the loved one in your arms and speak face to face.

A little bit of Jesus is never going to work. It's just not enough to live on. He is the Bread of Life. A little bit of the Holy Spirit only makes me hunger for more. Why do we starve ourselves? We (the Body of Christ) have been on a starvation diet, and we think we're fat. Why? Because we are fat on *hearing* good teaching, but very short on *learning*! Why are we not learning? Because we are not participating! In church some of us sit and listen with half our mind to what is being taught and the other half is thinking about what we want to accomplish later that day or where to have lunch after the last "amen." *We sit with our mind spiritually folded like our hands.* We take no action and make no place for the Holy Spirit Himself to teach us.

JUST THOUGHTS

My question: Lord, you reign over all, over all ideas, concepts, thoughts, and views, and over all principalities and powers. Why Lord? Why not just destroy all of us?

God's answer: It's all about choices. Yours! The destruction will come, but first you must yield to me while choice is still an option, for one day soon it will not be so. My rule is complete over everything except your will.

Most of us are still not ready to die to ourselves and live for Jesus. It's just too hard to give it all—our life completely. We can sing about giving it all to Jesus. We can even recite it. We may even want all of Him. However, we don't want to die.

I think believers may be chasing different facets of a beautifully cut diamond, the Jewel of Christ. And during the chase we are learning what each of the facets are; like to feel, to taste, and to experience. We move from one facet to the next in our desire to know the whole Gem, God the Father, God the Son, and God the Holy Spirit. We discover in Him all those things that are a part of us as individuals. God has more facets then can ever be counted or experienced—and the chase is worth every moment of our existence.

SUNRISE

Coming down the stairs one morning, I noticed the light coming through the blinds. It looked different this morning, and I couldn't wait to get over to the windows and open them. As I did, I saw a panoramic view of a beautiful sunrise, gloriously arrayed in colors of orange and pink with a touch of gold. I got my coffee and sat in front of the window. For the next half hour I communed with the Lord about the majesty and glory and artistic beauty of His creation.

I sensed that He was showing me some truths. He was speaking to me about prayer and the prayers that my wife and I and the church we attend have been praying. We have been calling out for a new and powerful visitation from the Lord. Just as I was about to get some understanding, up popped the sun. It was so bright that I could no longer look at it directly but had to avert my eyes so as to look at it from the side as protection from the strong beautiful rays. With this in mind I was filled with the revelation that if Jesus did show up in the fullness that we have been crying out for, we would not be able to stand the impact of the glory of His presence.

Then other truths came into view. The light filled the room where I was but I was aware that most of the other rooms in the house were still filled with darkness, hidden behind closed windows and doors. This time the truth was not as subtle. Only those rooms, those places in our lives that we open to the Son can be filled with His light. I also saw a picture of Moses hidden in the cleft of the rock, knowing full well that it was the mercy of the Lord that had put him there so he would not be destroyed by the full glory of the Lord as He passed by.

There is so much more of the Lord that we are not yet ready to see. It's an ever-increasing revelation that He wants for us, one that He wants us to enjoy as we walk along on life's journey. We want it all right now. "Give it to me," we cry, yet I believe that God in His infinite wisdom and grace wants to give us Himself in such a way and at such a pace that it will be good for us and our growth individually—and good for His corporate Church also. Another thought came to me about the other end of sunrise.

SUNSET

I saw it as a picture of His departing glory. I saw Moses with the veil over his face so not to allow the glory of the Lord to depart as he returned to the presence of sinful mankind. The glory of the Lord cannot remain on us in the presence of sin. Sin causes increasing darkness to sweep over us. True life begins in the light, and then the sun begins to set. As sin increases, darkness overwhelms and smothers our thinking and our life. The glory is no more.

What Is God Speaking to Me?

_____

_____

_____

_____

_____

_____

_____

_____

_____

_____

_____

_____

_____

_____

_____

_____

_____

_____

_____

_____

_____

_____

_____

CHAPTER 7

THE CALLING

(Who Do I Listen To? God or Man?)

I believe the call of God on our lives is very misunderstood and has caused great pain in many people. As Christians we are *all called* into the ministry, the *full time ministry*. The problem comes when hungry, fired up, excited people answer this call and believe that it can only mean one thing—pulpit ministry or one of the highly visible ministries such as evangelist or teacher or even apostle. The problem is interpretation! Isn't this where most of us get into trouble?

Motivation is great, and some people have a real gift to motivate others and to transmit excitement and urgency. However, this can be a problem as many who answer the broad call to minister answer the specific call to pastor. For some this means trying to walk in a size 9 shoe with a size 10½ foot. You may be able to carry it off, and it may even look good, but it will never be a right fit, and there will be pain.

Are you really called to the pulpit? Has God chosen you to go out (be sent) to preach the Gospel? To be the pastor of a church? To be an elder in the body? To be a worship leader or to be an evangelist?

Marlene and I have talked to many leaders who did believe or still believe that they were called into the ministry. They have a right heart (spirit) about them, yet they go out and are destroyed or devastated. Why, if they were called by God, has this happened to them?

Many times it's a case of not being rightly prepared, misguided interpretation, or in some cases just not hearing the voice of God for yourself. Some Christians were sent off to Bible college by some well-meaning pastor or leader but didn't really hear for themselves from God and got caught up in someone else's vision or dream. Bible college and seminary are tools and are very useful in studying the Word of God and understanding how to preach His Word. However, this is not the real preparation that is going to save you from the trials that are on the way.

Honest preparation will start with hard questions, such as: How is your private life? How is your marriage? (That one should probably be asked of your wife if one wants an honest answer.) How are your children? How are your emotions? Can you handle rejection and criticism? (There will be plenty of this to go around.) You will also be tested in any area of weakness you have. For example, your marriage will be tested, not once, but again and again. Your parenting skills will go through many challenges, and your social and political awareness will go through the fire. Everything that you are and hope to be will be thoroughly tested.

Unfortunately, most people go out way too soon, only to suffer in areas that they should never have had to suffer in. They get chewed up and spit out, and many of them are cast to the side, never to be whole again. Whose fault is this? God's? No. Let's look at the examples that He left for us to consider before going into "the ministry." Paul tells Timothy not to lay hands on a "novice" (see 1 Tim. 3:6). Look at Paul's life. Paul had many years in the "religious system" before being set aside (called) by Jesus on the road to Damascus. God put him through another 14 years of training before He was turned loose to share the Gospel with the world.

I think of "my" first church, and I shudder. I would never want to sit under a pastor who is pastoring his first church. Even today I'm afraid to listen to the tapes of those first few years I taught. It's not necessarily what I taught, but the arrogant and prideful way that I taught it. This was my church, and I couldn't be wrong, and woe to anyone who had the nerve to question me. After all, I was the one who had been called and had all the learning. Remember what God said about Paul's future: *"I will show him what he must suffer for me."* (See Acts 9:15-17.)

Now some of you who are reading this are asking this question: Why didn't someone warn me about all this before I went out? They probably did, but zeal has a way of blocking the ear from hearing, or you just weren't around people who were real enough to speak the truth, people who were able to be this honest with you. Anyone who speaks the truth takes the risk of being ridiculed for a lack of faith or unbelief. I believe that you can be honest and full of faith. No one wants to discourage you about going into the ministry or cause you to lose any of your zeal. The Lord knows you are going to need every bit of it.

Many senior pastors whom I have met have spent years building big walls around themselves, walls that they have erected for their own survival, and they don't want to risk letting them down for even a short time. It's kind of like being thrown into a lake to learn how to swim. "You'll be OK: just go for it." Drowning, drowning, drowning, without being seen. Sink or swim.

Each one of us must consider the cost before going to war, venturing near the water, or preaching from the pulpit. If it's really God calling you, then you won't wonder if He made a mistake when you are trounced on, beaten up, stoned by the church and left for dead—as was the case with Paul. No, Paul was truly called of God and endured and trusted God as he went through times of great stress and hardship.

If God has truly called you, no matter how much you want to run for cover in the back row of a big church, you won't be able to stay there. If you are truly called of God, you'll lick your wounds, and sooner or later you'll stop being angry with God and then stop feeling sorry for yourself and go back and do it all over again. This is not to say that you don't have good reason to give up and do something else with your life. You probably really did get hurt and you probably didn't deserve it. Hurts are real, and they are a real part of full-time service to God, whether you serve as a Christian worker or go into pulpit ministry.

The real call into the ministry is irrevocable. It may be seasonal. There may be breaks, but the hunger that God put deep down in your heart to be a servant won't cease. Passion and compassion are buried right under the pain, disappointment, and discouragement that you are hiding from, and they will keep trying to come to the surface over and over again. This may be a bit hard to hear now (depending on your current circumstance), but what you are going through was never meant to be a surprise to you. In reality, it is what you signed up for. It's just exactly what Jesus said would happen to those who choose to follow Him. What? You never checked the fine print before accepting the assignment?

Well, it's not too late. Let's go back and see what has been hidden from our eyes and why we are so eager to follow Jesus.

COMFORTABLE DISCOMFORT

Suffering is part of the price we pay for admission into this very special group. You don't become part of the ministry, or for that matter the Body of Christ, without it. You may open the door, but you won't go very far before you realize that this party is rough! You will get beat up by the unbeliever, the believer, and even the leadership that you are looking to for love and guidance. (See John 16 and 1 Peter 4:12-13; 5:10).

Why suffer? Because it's a part of relating with people. Jesus would not have had to suffer if it wasn't for the fallen state of people (1 Peter 2:19-23). Suffering is what you were called to! Things haven't changed that much. True, we now have salvation and the Word of God to live by. But there are still a few billion hurting people in this world. Where do they go for help? They seem to go toward those people who are just a few steps ahead of them in the process of reconciliation.

The Church is full of people who know they have problems. You have made the choice to work with hurting people. They come to the Church for help with things that they can't work out in their own lives.

You say you want to work only with nice people? Then you should go somewhere else. You say you don't want to work with hurting people but you want to follow Jesus? Well, that only works for about two weeks after salvation. Then He (Jesus) begins to bring people to you who are trying to work through the same things that you are learning to overcome. That's just the way it works. He saved us and brings healing to us so we can go and do the same for others. We are to comfort others with the comfort He gave us (see 2 Cor. 1:4-7). You can't truly follow Jesus without laying your life down over and over.

It just seems to happen, doesn't it? You are just getting over some major hurdle in your life and are beginning to see some victory, and here comes someone to test your new healing or commitment. Bam! They hit you with their stuff, and you have to choose how to respond. You have been taught, and hopefully learned a good way to respond, and now it's time to try it out. Want to or not, it's time. You can be knocked back and down, or you can grow with it and help them up. Both of you can move to a new level or not, and it seems that it is all in your hands. It's not really, but it seems that way. You see, Jesus knows when, where, and how to help us grow. And by now you should know that it won't be in your own timing!

I have a work of art hanging over my fireplace that is a very real reminder of where I was shortly before being converted. It is an oil painting of Christ on the Cross, and it keeps me from thinking of myself as more important than I ought. It keeps me humble, and reminds me of what Jesus had to overcome in my life (pride, arrogance, independence, and stubbornness), and how He brought me to my knees to see the pain one person can inflict on another. Lack of humility can be and has been a big problem with many pastors and leaders in the Church over the years.

BRINGING OUT THE WORST

For many years, I was a well-known hair stylist in Southern California. I worked in the beach areas of Newport Beach, Huntington Beach, Seal Beach, Costa Mesa, and inland in Santa Ana. While working in the Newport Beach salon, I took lessons from one of the best hair stylists in the country, and our salon had many celebrities who were regular customers. Movie stars, movie writers, and some very wealthy and prominent families would frequent our salon. We earned awards in style shows all over the region, and the salon was lined with trophies. There was a major stronghold for pride because we were good and we knew it.

As God would have it, it was in the Huntington Beach shop where I ran headlong into a lady who brought out the very worst in me. Sue was a Christian. You know, one of those who can't keep it quiet. She put Christian stickers on her mirror and witnessed to her clients. This drove me nuts. The conviction of who I was raised to be and who I was at this time in my life caused great turmoil in me, and I reacted in ways that were not kind. I was so far backslidden that it was hard for me to even see the starting line. I cursed Sue and ridiculed her. I put down her faith many times, and all this took place in front of the other stylist and all the customers. I caused her real pain and grief.

A couple of years later, when I was led kicking and screaming into the Kingdom of God, Sue was the first person the Lord led me back to so I could ask for forgiveness. I knew that the Lord forgave me, but I also knew that there was much unfinished business with Sue. When I asked her to forgive me, she was gracious, and she not only forgave me, but then she blessed me by painting this beautiful picture of Christ on the Cross for me. So now when I look up and see Him hanging there, it speaks to me of the grace of God, and of the way that I, as a Christian, need to respond to those who come against me. Over the years this painting has meant a lot to me, having a gift that screams "mercy" and "love," coming from two people who had to work very hard to walk that out.

Where we came from should *never* keep us from going where we are called to go. What He has done in us, He can and will do through us, if we will obey and go.

RECYCLED GOODS

While tent making in Northern California during the time when we planted a church, I was delivering home health care equipment. One day while making a delivery, I noticed a large pile of stuff that was being discarded. I saw a guitar case lying there and asked if I might have it for a friend of mine who needed a case for his guitar. The man said, "Well, let's go look at it," and when I pulled it off the pile and opened it, there was an old, very used and misused guitar inside. He said, "Oh, you can have that, too, if you want it." Well, I took it home and worked on it. I sanded down the fret board and all the fret bars. Then I took down the bridge and neck and reset the strings. Believe it or not, it works very well. I now use it as a testimony of my life—how Jesus found me on a junk heap and gave me life again. God is so good. He has restored me. And now when He wants to, He tunes me up and uses me to bring Him glory.

Note: To all of you pastors who have disenfranchised people who wouldn't go along with the program, I have a word for you: "Pray." Maybe they weren't rebellious. Maybe they saw your hands on the kingdom, molding it to your satisfaction, and they just couldn't buy into your views of how it was supposed to look. We (as pastors) have built our own kingdoms, surrounded with walls that, in reality, are designed to keep "our" people in, instead of keeping the enemy out. Remember the walls of Jericho? They were massive, and do we think that the God who brought down those walls so His people could move into what He had planned for their lives, could not bring down the paper thin walls that we have built around us? Do we for one minute believe that He is going to share His sovereignty over His creation with us? Not a chance! Jesus, as our model, is the author and finisher of our faith, not the controller and manipulator of our lives. We must break out of religious Christianity into the light of His will for His people.

Word: Again I find myself hearing from God in the shower. This time I am attending a meeting with a large group of Christian leaders. They were brainstorming about what the "new church" was going to look like. Some of you may not know that there is a big change coming and what we view as the "church" now is not what it will be in the future.

As this was going on, I stood up and began to speak out what I thought I was hearing from the Lord:

"The more you try to understand what shape the Church is going to take, the more it is going to remain the same because it will be formed by your hand and not mine. The new thing I am about to do, and am, in fact, doing now, is all about what I am doing and saying, and not what you think I am doing. Why? Because the more you know, the more you try to control, and as I have said in My Word, I am the head, and you are the body. The head leads and the body follows. That is the way I created it, and that is the way I want it to function."

I believe this has a lot to do with the vision about the room full of lambs, mentioned in Chapter 3. The lambs have no clue because the shepherds have no clue. We just can't seem to keep our hands off of what God is doing. The fear of being out of control is so great that it drives the leaders to make the rules. Somehow we have the idea that if we allow God to be in charge, we will have nothing but chaos in the assembly. This couldn't be further from the truth.

What Is God Speaking to Me?

_____

_____

_____

_____

_____

CHAPTER 8

THE HIDING PLACE

(Lord, How Do I Deal With This Pain?)

I must admit before going very far into this chapter that I ran— I took refuge in the world of work. When I left "my" first church, I thought my life was over. I thought there was nothing left that I could do for the Lord. Being a pastor was it, and if I couldn't do that, then what was the use in existing? I was a mess, and I needed help. In His time, the Lord directed my restoration.

THE HIDING PLACE

1. Where is your hiding place?

2. What cave do you run into to hide?

3. Where do you go when you fear an attack is coming?

4. What type of place do you hide in?

Answering these questions doesn't disqualify you from the calling that God has on your life. But you also need to ask yourself this question: 5. Will you live there, or are you just a visitor? Many people run and hide and then regroup to come out fighting. However, most learn after time passes that hiding is far less painful than fighting. You cannot suffer defeat at the hands of the enemy if he cannot find you. This, of course, is a lie, and then the real defeat comes from way down deep inside of you when you realize that you are no longer an effective part of the army of God.

The simple truth is that many pastors and church leaders hide from their people, the very ones they are called to love. They build in insulation in the form of elders, assistants, secretaries, and all sorts of ways that seem as if they are too busy doing God's work to get involved with the everyday lives of the people. We can even find Scriptures to justify our case and ease or hold off the pain that we are just plain afraid of experiencing. Many are afraid or unwilling to be hurt anymore. Are you a prisoner in your own castle? Is this you?

Many pastors and leaders are wounded or burned out and want to protect themselves. Protect themselves from what? People. The same people Jesus died for and called you to comfort, teach, and serve.

All people are wounded. Don't be fooled by the ones who look as if they have it all together. They just hide their fears better than others. All of them are capable of hurting you. All of them have their own set of questions about life, death, love, the Bible, and the Church. And sooner or later they will get around to asking you to answer them. We will never have all the right answers, and we learn very quickly that we try to answer questions when we honestly don't have a clue. We disappoint people.

We make mistakes. We try to look good, and we will fail. People want answers, and we want to please. This is a recipe for disaster.

Who did Jesus die for? Them! Us! You cannot find a group of people to pastor who don't have hidden problems or a hidden agenda.

If you look at the leaders in the Bible, it will scare you out of being a pastor. Isaiah, David, Moses, Peter, James, John, Paul. They all ran, they hid, they failed, they were murdered—and they were *called*. Why did they do it? Why do we want to do it?

Believers are hungry to share the Gospel of Jesus Christ. We who speak the Gospel are all to be called stupid if this Gospel is not true. Those who preceded us knew the true God and could not help but speak about Him, and they are our examples.

There is a song that says this very well. "The Spirit of the Sovereign Lord is upon you because He has anointed you to preach good news." These words are based on Isaiah 61:1-7—a passage that proves to be a source of great pain and a reminder of the calling on my life.

FOR I AM COMPELLED TO PREACH

We were preparing for the 10th anniversary of the Vineyard Christian Fellowship in Anaheim, California. Someone had made very beautiful banners that were hung in the main sanctuary, and one pastor's wife and I were walking down the aisle to read them when we came upon a banner with Isaiah 61:1-7 on it. Please remember that I was in the Vineyard trying to get healed from my first church when I read this banner. I heard the

Lord say that it was time to go out again. I literally ran out of the church building and out into the parking lot screaming, "No, no, no, not again, Lord." But as you might have guessed, He had His way.

If we really want to know why we feel this unending desire to pastor or lead (serve and minister), then we must look to the same calling as that of Isaiah and understand that God has placed this burden on the hearts of many and that it is not just a good thought or idea. This is a lifetime call that may or may not have seasons to it. "*Yet when I preach the gospel, I cannot boast, for I am compelled to preach. Woe to me if I do not preach the gospel*" (1 Cor. 9:16).

It's just not safe to relate with people or God. You simply don't know what they are going to do; however, God did not call us to play it safe. People will transgress our boundaries, and rightly so, for God has placed this in the hearts of His people. If we allow God to take back His Church, He as our model will also cross over the lines, borders, and boundaries that we have set. If we are not relying on Him for the answers to the questions of life, then I feel sorry for us.

In the same way, He didn't call us to lead because we knew the way. It should be new territory for each person whom God puts into our lives, for He created each one of us as individuals. No two are alike. In the same way, each church body is different. Surely, they all need some of the same things: teaching, love, compassion, mercy, and direction. But the meal that we serve to meet these needs should be seasoned uniquely for them. The only way I know how to achieve this is by the leading of the Holy Spirit, and that means we must allow God to be God in our midst.

What Is God Speaking to Me?

_____

_____

_____

_____

_____

_____

_____

_____

_____

_____

_____

_____

_____

CHAPTER 9

ARE YOU REALLY GOD?

As I was sitting in the living room of some friends one night worshiping the Lord, some thoughts came to mind. As songs were playing on a CD about our identity and our inheritance, along with some of the promises of God for our lives, the following came to me. "All this (identity, inheritance, promises) must happen or the Word of God is not true, and God is a liar. And if that is the truth, then we are fools and the most stupid of all people, because we have placed all our hopes and dreams and even visions in the hands of a God who does not exist."

As I've continued to think about these thoughts it's clear that we choose to believe that the God of history is still the God of today, and we have faith in the God of all creation, the God of the Red Sea and the Great Flood, the God who raised Jesus Christ from the dead. He is the Lord of today, the Lord of power, the Lord of healing, the Lord of mercy and grace, and the Lord of salvation.

Now from my way of thinking, this means that if I choose to believe that the God of the Bible is real and that Jesus Christ is God the Son (the second person of the Trinity) then my life must reflect this belief in tangible ways. Faith in those wonderful promises is of the highest value. For if I don't believe in the promises of God then I don't believe that He is who He says He is and that He is capable of bringing them to pass in my life and even desires to do so. I don't believe that this is automatic. However, it is the same faith that I used to believe in Him that must be put to use in believing that a promise is being fulfilled in my life. "It takes faith to please God." That's the faith it takes to believe in Him.

We cannot believe in the God of the Bible and not believe all the promises of the Bible unless you have chosen to have selective belief, and man is certainly capable of this, as proven in the dispensation doctrine. I know that there are times and ends of times in the Bible, but I don't think that claiming beginnings and endings of the activity of the Holy Spirit is a very good thing to do. This, of course, is man's effort to understand the things of God and place them in a form that man can control. Healing is considered in much the same way. If a person does not get healed then we find it necessary to create a doctrine to cover such an event. In effect, we are saying that God didn't really mean what He said or some mistake was made by His secretary when writing out the rules.

God does not need to explain His actions to us! I have come to the place in my personal belief system that acknowledges the reality that God's ways do not need to be explained away if I don't understand them. Ours is to speak, obey, believe, and stand. The rest is up to Him and how He chooses to respond—or not. Believing is not an option for Christians. That is where we start with God, and we are supposed to keep growing on from there.

"*Trust in the Lord with all your heart and lean not to your own under-standing*" (Proverbs 3:5). Of course, this Scripture is only good for those who believe that the Bible is the *Word of God*. Trusting in the Lord God would be foolish for someone who doesn't believe that He is real and alive and wants us to trust in Him.

What does "I believe in God" mean? Does it only mean that I believe that there *is* a God? From man's point of view, that could mean anything: a sun god, a rock god, a carved god of wood or iron or whatever! Does it mean one God or many gods? Is He the God of all creation or the god of earth? Is mother earth, god?

Who is the God you trust in?

FIRE IN HIS EYES AND A SWORD IN HIS HAND

Can we look into the face of the "God of Now"?

I'm sitting in a home meeting worshiping, and these thoughts come to me. We cry out to look into the face of the awesome living God, but can we? Are we willing to see Him the way He looks now with fire in His eyes and His hair white as snow. Will His feet of bronze cause fear in us and cause us to run, or can we still see the loving, compassionate "Lamb of God"? Do we get confused about who He is and what He is like now? He is awesome in beauty and fearful in majesty.

If we don't know Him, He is a contradiction! On one hand He is "One like a Lamb Slain" and on the other, "One with fire in His eyes and a sword in His hand, and riding a white horse." (See Revelation 5:6; 1:14.)

Scripture tells us that He died as a lamb and was raised as a mighty conquering warrior. He sits at the right hand of God, always making intercession for us; yet He lives in Heaven and makes His home in my heart. Our God comes like a mighty, rushing wind, and yet, *in Him* there is peace like a river.

Think about it! What is your God like, and where is He right now?

He is the God of Now!

What Is God Speaking to Me?

_____

_____

_____

_____

_____

_____

_____

_____

_____

_____

_____

_____

_____

_____

_____

_____

_____

_____

_____

_____

_____

_____

CHAPTER 10

WHAT'S HAPPENING TO THE CHURCH?

IT'S important to speak to you about the state of the Church today—about religious Christianity. I can hear Jesus' words as He stands on a bluff overlooking the City of David. "Oh, Jerusalem, Jerusalem, how I have longed to hold you and embrace you" (paraphrased Matt. 23:37).

I have some of those same feelings. Oh, Church of God, where are you? How I long to be in your midst. I want to be a part of a church that honestly believes that God inhabits His people. I want to hang out with those who believe that God has chosen to dwell not only *with* them but *in* them. This is not knowledge but rather revelation.

Where are the "do or die" standards of the Church, the people of God? Where is the understanding that He may return at any moment?

I can remember when we were young pre-martyrs ready to give our lives, ready to stand up for the principles of God to any situation that came our way. We would rather die than compromise the Word of God. Serving in His army was not an option. It was all; it was everything! I am missing this. I find myself longing for this *type* of Christianity again where we would line up at the doors of the churches trying to get the best seats, hungry for the Lord and His Word. When the doors opened, people rushed into the buildings because they hungered for an encounter with the Living God. "*These things I remember as I pour out my soul: how I used to go with the multitude, leading the procession to the house of God, with shouts of joy and thanksgiving among the festive throng*" (Psalm 42:4).

It seems that nowadays when we hear of a church like this, we (the larger body of Christ) work very hard to make sure *our* people don't become like-minded with those *super believers*. We find ways of putting down their zeal, careful not to sound ungodly, and putting out their fire because we may lose our jobs or the reputation we have worked so hard to build up. These thoughts and actions are demonic! This is a tactic straight from the ruler of darkness. Criticize every real move of the Holy Spirit so the people look like weirdoes, and then those who practice conservative Christianity look "right."

We have become (as a whole) *a la carte Christians* with a *salad bar mentality*! Some of us view Christianity as a giant smorgasbord, and we go down the line looking for the things that suit our own palate. Oh, look, doesn't that look tasty today. Watch out for that one; it's much too rich for me. Or maybe this one: "That was Old Testament, and it is not for today." I am not advocating that you go to one of these places and try to put some of everything on your plate, although I have tried this many times.

Think with me. It's the Word of God that I am speaking of. *What part of it would not be good for me?* The Old and the New Testaments contain the very heart of God. His message, His will, and yes, His Words. If we believe that the Bible is the inspired Word of God, then it is *all* designed as good food, to nourish and build up those who eat of it! Come on, eat your fill and I'll guarantee that you will never get too full. Then let the Holy Spirit direct you as to what to eat for each meal.

We as Christians are as guilty as any of the Pharisees in the day of Jesus. They had and still have their Talmud, all the laws and requirements they built into the Jewish religion, based on the Law of Moses or the Torah. We are guilty of the same thing, only ours is not so organized that we have it all down in one place or that it is the same in every church.

THOU SHALT NOT

Each Christian church has its own Talmud. By that, I mean those things that the leadership considers acceptable in their congregation. Many of these things have emerged from someone's idea of what they consider to be OK, based on a set of their own standards, such as women cannot wear slacks to church. I know this is an old tradition, but I just recently saw this dress code listed on the front door of a church. It excluded women from attending church while wearing pants. Find that one in the Bible!

Don't eat, don't taste, don't smell, or whatever. Some say that if you do this or that, you are guilty of some sin. Of course, this is meant to control you and to conform you to the standards that they believe, but it is not sin. Many things that we label sin are not called sin in the Bible. Why do we come up with these things?

Certainly they did not come from God, but we blame them on Him. Drinking alcohol is a big one. Oh, I know that we are admonished not to do anything to stumble a brother, but if he is stumbled by a false doctrine, then that doctrine must be changed. Yes, I know that we are also admonished not to stay long over our drink or not to be given to it, but isn't that true with almost everything? Overindulgence of anything is wrong lest it be on God or His Word. You can even overindulge in ministry. The bottom line is that people in the Bible drank, and it wasn't grape juice. This may or may not be of value, but to write books about the sin of drinking alcohol and to make church doctrine about it when there is no biblical foundation is too much for me consider seriously.

How about the tithe? I know this is an untouchable tenet of the Church and like many of you I have struggled with this principle, too. But it's something that each person needs to look at and see if they believe this is *New Testament* or not. When I say New Testament, I am not saying that I believe the Old Testament has been done away with or is to be ignored and that we need not pay attention to what it has to say. The entire Bible is valid and relevant today. God did not change His views on things from the old to the new. All they had in Jesus' day was the Old Testament. Jesus used it, and He said that not one jot or tittle would pass away. Yes, fulfillment can be found in Jesus Christ. But what is being fulfilled? How do we know the heart of God and what pleases Him if we do away with what He has spoken?

The tithe, I believe, is how people support their pastor and church. Giving your resources is how we meet the needs of others. According to the Word of God the *tithe* belongs to God and *giving* is treated in a different manner. Giving comes after the tithe, and it is to be done cheerfully. Giving can take on many forms, such as the programs you sponsor. It's true that there has been, and still is, financial abuse in the church but we cannot ignore what the Word of God says just because we are afraid it may not be used in the right way or because we simply don't want to participate. Can we? Dare we?

HAND-ME-DOWNS AND LEFTOVERS

I am including this story here because it has much to say about tithing. Being one of the original latchkey kids of 1941 (no parental supervision), I did many things that could have cost me my life. They cause so much pain, that when telling my mother about some of them many years later she could not believe them.

My parents were divorced when I was about 1 year old, and all the children lived with my mother, who, of course, had to work. She worked a defense job at Lockheed Aircraft Company in the San Fernando Valley of California. I was the youngest of four children, and we were raised in childcare centers while Mom worked, and most of the time we were left to our own devices. We ate lead-based paint (at the time who knew?), played with mercury batteries from hearing aids (the mercury made pennies and dimes so shiny), and of course we ate from aluminum pans, and as I said before, we had little or no supervision. Many of the other things we did, you don't need to know. All this to say that my mother had her hands full; and for many of those years after the war, my mother had no clue where her children were or what they were doing or for that matter where the next meal was coming from.

Somehow we always had what we needed—we also got the most out of what we did have. Because I was the fourth child, when clothes and other things got handed down to me, they were a bit worn out. But one thing Mom did do was tithe. I know for sure that my mother has tithed as long as I have been alive, which is more than 65 years. Marlene and I have tithed for more than 30 years, and we feel that the Lord has always taken very good care of us.

With all the problems centered around money in the Church today, I think that if God's people would just learn the lessons of giving to God and not to man—and not be so paranoid about what the pastor wears or drives or what blessings he receives—then most tithing problems would simply go away. We will always have people in the Church who abuse the privilege of the office from our way of thinking. They are not your problem, unless you have become the head of your church and you have taken the place of the Holy Spirit. Whether or not tithing is what some call *New Testament* and I am supposing they mean by that "for today," giving certainly is! Even Jesus told the religious leaders of His day that they should continue the tithe (see Luke 11:41).

The people of each church build in their own form of what they see as the Christian lifestyle, much of which has no Bible base, just like The Apostles' Creed. How many versions of this are there? I have personally seen several. I call this *personal pollution* of the Word of God. I am not opposed to tithing, but tithing, like all the rest of God's Word, must be personal.

I can remember trying to make sure everyone who was a part of my first church was conforming to my views of what the Bible had to say. And yes, I built in my own views and rules. If you didn't do it my way, you couldn't be a part of the leadership of the church. And God help you if you came against any of my teachings or even shared a different perspective than mine. Our views are so narrow, based mostly on what is comfortable for us what we can control and keep in line.

Most pastors I have known are secure only if people agree with them. I thank God for leading me to a church where the pastor encourages people to think for themselves. This causes people to grow and be developed by the Holy Spirit and not by someone else's opinion. But what if they do disagree with you or what you teach as the true Word of God? You are not their God, nor is anyone else who skipped dying on a cross or creating something like the world.

TODAY'S CHURCH IS SICK

One of the symptoms of this sickness has a name: *Christian divorce!* I do not want to talk about divorce in general, so I'll just say a few words about Christian divorce. How can these words even go together? Isn't that an oxymoron?

This topic is painful for me. Some of my good friends have succumbed to this plague. And that is exactly what it is—a dark, dirty, deadly plague that is spreading rapidly within the Body of Christ. What's the deal? When did it become OK for Christians to get divorced?

I have heard that there are polls which show that Christian divorce has now outpaced non-Christian divorce. The numbers have been edging up for some time, but now it is said that more Christians get divorced than the people we are sent to minister to. These are tragic circumstances!

You might ask, and rightly so, "How could this be?" I've heard several answers, but they deal with the wrong issues.

Divorce is only a symptom of what's going on in the Body of Christ today and in the lives of its individuals. Generally, divorce happens because one or both partners are more interested in serving themselves than they are in serving God. It's a heart issue (see Matt. 19:1-11). Oh, I know that there are some situations that will not work out without a whole lot of change by both husband and wife. If both parties are Christian then there is a chance—or at least there is supposed to be.

I remember when my wife and I were newly born Christians, and our marriage looked like a train wreck, a true disaster. We had both come into the Body of Christ with broken lives. Each of us had been divorced, and both of us had young children of our own. Our chosen spouses had left us for greener pastures. We, to say the least, were both very wounded and angry people.

Once while we were counseling with a pastor, one on one side and one on the other (he looked like he was watching a ping-pong match), he said, "I don't know even with Jesus if your marriage can be saved." We fought over everything! I would say, "No woman is going to tell me what to do." The truth is that I was still rebelling against my single-parent (Mother) upbringing and the pain of a shattered marriage. Marlene on the other hand, had a real problem with men, and so she would say, "No man is going to run my life." The only man who said "I love you" to her had left her for another woman. She never heard "I love you" from her earthly father until he was dying. Then he also left her.

This all happened 34 years ago, and we are still together. That pastor was wrong. But a lot had to change. One thing that hindered us was that we came into the Body of Christ when there was a great emphasis placed on submission, or "the s word" as it came to be called. Women had to be in submission to their own husbands, and boy, did I play that one for all it was worth.

KINGSHIP

I liked kingship, for I seldom if ever had to be wrong. If Marlene didn't go along with the church and/or what I believed, then it was off to the elders we would go. My wife was so spiritually abused by me and by the church that it is only by the grace of God alone that she loves Jesus or me today. One of the main things that helped bring us through this very difficult time was that old teaching on the triangle where God is at the top, my wife on one side, and me on the other side. As long as both of us were earnestly seeking after God, then we were both being drawn closer and closer together. It takes time, but it works.

Then one day, my wife took a class taught by Gloria Thompson and Carol Wimber. It was called "Free to Be." It almost killed us.

My wife discovered her identity apart from me. I had more or less been taught that she didn't have a separate identity apart from me. Boy, was I wrong. Well, in the end, it was one of the best things that could have happened to us. It changed everything. I now have a wife with a voice and a personal identity, and now I cannot use guilt to manipulate her, to make her go along with me. She actually thinks. (Oh, how dangerous.)

I had to come to grips with the fact that the day of "my kingship" was over. I was now being called to serve her as Christ served the Church and gave Himself up for her, Oh, what a change! How do I even begin? This new arrangement will kill us!

I was afraid she would take advantage of her new identity, and, of course, she did. Am I a man or a mouse? The old walls had to come down. I had to become a servant leader in our home, and the truth is that this is an ongoing lesson. We had so many years of wrong teaching to overcome, but the end result is much better. Someone said the other day that they had been married for more than 20 years and that the last 10 years had been great. It takes time for us to get this right.

My wife had to learn that she needed to go to God for herself and not to depend on me to have all the right answers. Together we are *one*. How do you separate one without tearing it apart? You can't. It's simply impossible. But separately, we both had our own relationships with Jesus to work out.

Now you understand that my wife's story will be different than mine, but the undeniable truth is that we gave our pastors a real workout. Even though I don't agree with everything they did or taught, I know that we would not be together without their love for Jesus and for us. They paid a great price for our marriage, and I am grateful to them for that and so much more.

Marriage is work! Hard work! It's a lot of hard work! If there is one subject that the Bible is clear about, it's marriage and divorce. God does not waste His words, and from Genesis to Revelation, He never changes His mind on this point. He does not like nor does He condone divorce. Yes, I know, He does give you an out for your spouse's unfaithfulness. And should you make the mistake (sin) of marrying an unbeliever, you may have an out if that unbeliever wants out on his own and not because you have made life so difficult that he or she wants to leave. But divorce was not God's plan from the beginning.

Divorce is a spiritual issue, because the spirit of divorce is in the land, and it does not belong to God. We are always divorcing God and going after other gods, so it is in the natural because we want to be satisfied rather than to satisfy. He said that we are one flesh (see Genesis 2:24), and one cannot be separated and still be whole. I don't care what kind of new math you use; it just can't be done. We become one flesh, the Bible says, and as I have just said, the only way to separate one is to cut or tear it apart. The result of this is years of pain for yourself and your family.

I don't know what you have been told, but the truth of the matter is that it is never over. Your mind will never let you forget even with the most wonderful new love you can find. I speak from the pain of the divorce experience, and there is always going to be reaping from what we sowed. Look at it from this point of view. The Bible says that marriage is the mystery of the Church. Now we know that the relationship with Jesus always needs to be worked on from our side, don't we? It takes a real effort to keep our hearts right. The work never stops, nor can it be taken for granted. Look at your life and what you would like to have in a relationship with the Lord, then count the cost of what you think it might take to achieve that. Now realize that this effort is what it will take to have a godly marriage that lasts! You can never take that for granted.

In both of these relationships (ours with God and ours with our spouse) the price is too high to allow it to erode into an empty shell of what it was or what it could be. It is only the foolishness in our hearts that tells us that *everything is all right; you don't have to work at this.*

The price is too high to let complacency in our relationship with the Lord or with our mates develop. It only leads to disaster.

I am completely convinced that there is nothing that cannot be healed, restored, or fixed, whether it is a marriage, financial problems, relationships, or any other type of problem, *if* all parties are working toward a right relationship with Jesus Christ. Anything less is not enough.

Salvation takes only an acceptance. Relationship takes time and effort and the rest of our lives.

Think about any good relationship that you have or have had in the past. It didn't just happen. You had to work at it. You have to give, serve, listen, communicate, and give up a selfish attitude. Remember all those long phone calls, the dinner dates, and flowers? You had to woo her and make her more important than yourself in order to win that relationship. With the Lord this works very well. You pursue Him, and He comes in like a flood. A broken marriage makes becoming all we can be in Christ all the more difficult, but it's not impossible if we will trust Him to heal the hurt and believe that it was not God's fault nor His will that you and your spouse were torn in two.

WORD: HEAR THE HEART OF GOD

What is this thing you're doing in My name? If I was merely a man, and I lived among you with your laws and your beliefs, I could sue you for false representation. You use My name to curse people. You use My name to gossip and hurt one another. In what part of Me did you find that? Does not My Word say that sweet water and salt water, blessing and curses, should not come out of the same cistern? The idea that I left you with, was that you were to be representations of God to this world. You are acting as if this were a *part-time job* and not a *life-long work*. When are you going to get serious about the work I left you to do—to 'Go ye into all the world and preach the gospel to every creature?' Have you forgotten again who you are? Why I made you? Why I gave you life again and did not give you what you deserve?

I can hear Him saying, "Oh, foolish generation, when are you going to come forth as I called forth Lazarus? I've freed you, but not so you can forget Me or who I have called you to be."

VISION

While we were in Albuquerque, New Mexico one weekend visiting with my daughter and my newest granddaughter, we were at our friend's home, and as we began to minister to them, we put on a CD by Don Potter. One song is very real to our lives and ministry, so as I started singing this song, I had a vision. I was in a church in an old Western town back in the 1800s. The church was at the end of a dirt side street just off the main street of town. As people came into the church, there was a shelf with pegs under it where the men would hang their guns while they were in the service, but today the people who came had chains on their arms and shackles around their ankles. As they entered, they took the chains and shackles off and hung them on the gun rack. As they took their seats, the scene changed to a modern church of today. When the service was over and the people began to leave, they would stop at the gun rack and retrieve their chains and shackles and put them back on and then leave.

The Lord showed me that this is what His Church has been doing for centuries. They come to church and experience an hour or two of what they perceived as freedom; then they walk back into bondage again. They believe that freedom is at the church, and that is why they look forward to going there once a week. There were a very small number of people who escaped the building without reclaiming their chains, and all I could see of those who were now free was the dust going up the street. I was impressed by how fast they could go when they were no longer in bondage.

Recently the Lord had me visit this same church again in another vision. This time the church was surrounded by what, at first glance, looked like sheriffs in old-time Western clothes. They were encouraging people to come in, yet in reality they were there to keep the people from leaving without their chains of bondage. They seemed to represent some kind of authority. They were stationed at each opening (windows and doors) and even on the roof. From where I was I could see the whole picture. As I moved around, I could see that they appeared to be only half human, because when I saw them from the rear, I could see that each one of them had black leathery wings and black shiny bodies. I couldn't tell whether they were on the backs of these people or whether they were one.

As I reflect on the sheriffs and the meaning of their authority, I think they represent the authority that we as believers give the enemy to speak into our lives. You say, "Wait a minute; I don't give him authority to speak into my life!" Yes you do, every time you entertain an ungodly thought instead of demanding it to leave. Those thoughts don't come from God, so you figure it out. There are only two kingdoms. One belongs to God and one belongs satan. As far as I know, it's *either* one or the other. There is no *neither* world.

What Is God Speaking to Me?

_____

_____

_____

_____

_____

_____

_____

_____

_____

_____

_____

_____

_____

_____

_____

_____

CHAPTER 11

NOW WE'RE TALKING

GIFTS OF THE SPIRIT
AND ETERNAL SECURITY

I believe that eternal security is a half-truth that has been put upon the Body of Christ. Whether you are a Calvinist or an Arminian, you need to do all you can to assure that your own ongoing relationship with God is current and vital.

The eternal security half-truth gives a person a false sense of security. Then when you hook that with the grace and the mercy of God you have a formula for excess which can lead you into sin, and then into death, both spiritual and physical (see James 1:14-15). Can you tell me where the fear of God is in this way of thinking? By fear I don't mean that we are to be afraid of God, but we are to be filled with a reverence and an awe of God. Otherwise, why obey Him at all? He has saved us, and His grace will keep us in His good stead. Where is the dependence on God for direction for your life? This doctrine says to me that I can go out and boogie all I want and there will be no consequences for it.

Eternal security is a difficult subject. I asked Jesus Christ into my life at a very young age. In fact, it was at Billy Graham's first or second crusade at the Hollywood Bowl about 1946-47. With a little math, you can see this was a long time ago. I believed and was taught that I was saved forever—eternally secure. I believed that Jesus was God's son and that He died on the Cross for my sins. And because these are the most important doctrines of salvation, I was saved.

As I grew up things got kind of messed up in me, and I became confused about this and life in general. Without a dad as a role model, I turned to the heroes of World War II and the early cowboys on TV. And then, of course, there were my two older brothers. Great role models!

I was taught that if I wanted to be eternally secure, the best way was for me to follow Jesus. If you faithfully do this, then you will be eternally secure. This seemed impossible for me to do at that time in my life. It wasn't until much later (age 31) that I made a real, true commitment to the Lord. Until then, I still had the understanding in my mind of Jesus as the Son of God and that He was watching for me to sin so He could give me a licking (much like my mother and stepfather). I gave Jesus a lot to look at, and I had to sin very deliberately, for His face was always right there in front of me. He ruined many a fun time for me. Did you know that sin is fun? (I learned that from Pinocchio.) Of course, it always leads to one type of death or the other, either spiritual or physical. I spent many years doing my best to be as bad as I could. After I got out of the Navy and a very difficult divorce, I remarried and found that I wasn't very good at marriage this time, either.

My wife Marlene got saved (remember that angel back in Chapter 4) at a "Jews for Jesus" meeting that my sister took her to. Not long after Marlene got saved, I really got saved. Now I know that this may not line up with your doctrine, but, to tell you the truth, I doubt that if I would have died before my *real conversion* that I would have gone to Heaven, although Jesus did make it much more difficult for me to sin. All those years that I ran from him, He was with me every step of the way. I had to look at His face while my flesh did what it wanted to do. My soul was in the place where my spirit should have been, and all the decisions I made were of the flesh.

I really don't know how it all works, not that I haven't studied it, yet there are still unknown areas when it comes to whether or not I was saved when I first asked Jesus into my life at about 6 years old, or whether it was as an adult when I cried out to Him in my living room. However, one thing I do know is that as long as I follow hard after my Lord Jesus and believe in Him and what He did on the Cross for me, then what I believe about eternal security is not what's going to get me into Heaven—it's my relationship with Him that counts.

SPIRITUAL GIFTS

We are to work out our own salvation with fear and trembling. It's much like the gifts of the Spirit. Yes, you can be saved without functioning in the use of the gifts of the Spirit, but why would anyone want to?

To be eternally secure is to have a vital, ongoing relationship with Jesus our Lord. Otherwise, all you are trying to accomplish is to escape hell, and you never get around to answering these questions: Why did He pay so much, at such a great price, for me? What does He want from me? How can I participate in what He is doing today? What's my purpose in all this?

How can we be vital in the army of God without the right view of who we are and what equipment we have in order to carry out the Great Commission? Send a fighting man into battle without his weapons, and what you have is a casualty, and how many there are! Ask the Lord to let you *see the Body of Christ through His eyes* if you dare.

In World War II, Germany far outpaced the Americans in technology. The Germans had the superior weapons development. However, we were able to keep them from using it to their utmost ability. How could this be? We cut off their fuel supplies and hindered their ability to manufacture their weapons. We struck at their supply lines and delivery systems. This has been a large part of satan's plan, who has done everything possible to stop the use of the gifts of the Spirit. The gifts are weapons given to us by God to carry on the work He has set aside for you and me to do until His return.

Jesus modeled these gifts for us, demonstrating their proper use and the power that they have to change lives, and then said, "Now you go out and do the same things in my place." To counter this, the enemy established a huge anti-gift campaign, knowing full well that if he could stop the flow of our warfare weapons (cutting off the supply lines), then he could muzzle the power of Christianity. It has almost worked. Many churches look with disdain at the use of the gifts of the Spirit today. They interpret the Bible to say that gifts stopped at the end of the apostolic age. This is nothing but a lie from satan to cause confusion and doubt, which he hopes will bring an end to the use of the gifts of the Spirit.

The people of the world who don't know Jesus are living in this day and age as a people without hope. They don't see personal victory in their futures. When you look closely at them, there is a vacant look in their eyes. They have no reason to hope in a future that goes beyond the few years we have here on earth. I hear questions in their speech and their hearts: So what? Who cares? What's up with that? They already know that "things" are not the answer to what life is all about. Because they have no answers or hope, life has lost its importance and has little or no meaning to them without the promise of a future.

As those who claim to know the truth, we have lost the sharp edge to that truth, because we too have been tainted with the same lies. Oh, yes, the enemy is more subtle with us. The questions he puts to us are more along the lines of accusations and doubt—that the use of the gifts of the Spirit only bring abuse. The enemy uses pride—you look different from the rest of us. You'll look stupid, and people will laugh at you. Oh yes, then there is this one that always has the sting of truth: People who use the gifts of the Spirit think that they are better than everyone else. You don't need them to be saved, so why set yourself up to be rejected? And satan goes on and on destroying people's desire to use their gifts.

It seems as if more and more Christians are spending more and more time trying to figure out why they don't have to live righteously. Then they are trying to figure out how righteous living is to be walked out. It's all a part of the campaign to disarm the troops and it has worked quite well.

The gifts of the Spirit are vital to the ongoing existence of Christianity. They are given to us to give life to others, to encourage and build up, to give hope where hope has lost its power, and to see the power and involvement of God in our everyday lives. Christianity without the gifts is much like a military tank without gas or ammunition. It cannot carry out the purpose it was made for, and neither can the Christian who is not sharing the gifts with the Body of Christ. This is why the enemy fights so hard to defeat the use of them.

Some will argue that for centuries Christians have been going out into the mission field who do not believe in the use of the gifts for today. Bless them. For the many success stories we've heard about, we know of many more who found themselves ill-equipped and became victims instead of conquerors. The Bible is much more clear about the use of the gifts of the Spirit than it is about the cessation of them.

What Is God Speaking to Me?

_____

_____

_____

_____

_____

CHAPTER 12

CRUSH TIME

(We Have Been Lied To)

W E, the Body of Christ, have been lied to far too often. First we were lied to by satan (the father of lies), then by the world, then by our flesh, and finally by the Church. What are we going to do about this? Do we just roll over and hope in eternal security and the grace of God? No! We must wage war against the unseen enemy and also against our own souls. Our soul has been lied to about who we are and what that means, to the point where we believe little bits and pieces of these lies. This has had a tremendous negative effect on how we walk out our lives as Christians and how this is walked out in the Church. Religious Christianity is the result.

As I was reading in John 17 verses 5 and 22, this thought came to me: Could Jesus be showing us again just what is available for us? As Jesus prayed, I saw that we could interchange our name with His: "Father, Jesus has given us the glory that you gave Him, now Father glorify me in your presence with the glory we (I) had with you in the garden when you created me" (our beginning) (my paraphrase). "*And now Father, glorify Me* [Jesus] *in Your presence with the glory I had with You before the world began,*" (John 17:5). "*I have given them* (us) *the glory that You gave Me, that they may be one as We are one*" (John 1:22).

As example: Many years ago the Lord showed me some truth from the logo of a Christian fellowship we were a part of at the time. It shows a bunch of grapes on a vine. Many times as I focused on this picture, one grape would fall away from the rest of the bunch. As an artist, I drew this repeatedly. The grape would fall into a winepress and then out of the base would come the wine. I know the Lord was saying many things to me from this illustration—things to do with what He wanted to make of me (us) and the crushing that it will take to bring them to pass.

Many years later I now see some of the deep changes that this process has brought about in me. Part of this is the squeezing out of the strong religious spirit that had such a stronghold in my life.

I ask many Christians what is going on in their lives and their Church, and I get a response something like: "I really don't know, but it's just not the same. Something is going on, because it is not very comfortable in here anymore."

PRAISE THE LORD! IT IS *CRUSH TIME.*

If you have not lived in "wine country," you may not understand the importance of this term or of this time of year. It's harvest time, and all other priorities are put aside. The grapes are picked and immediately dumped into the crushing machine. As you travel around the area, you can see the piles of grape skins and seeds all over the vineyards. And almost everywhere you go, the sweet smell of wine hangs in the air. For several years, I worked in Napa, California, living in Santa Rosa and daily driving throughout the wine country on my delivery route. This is the heart of California's wine country.

In order for the wine to be made pure and to bring out the very best taste (not sour,) the grapes must be picked at the right time, separated from the skin and seed, and then strained and purified. Most of the grape is discarded, and only the juice is left.

I believe that God is in the process of producing the best wine (vital Christians) for these last times. While He carries out this work in you and me, we will go though many different processes. All of the different stages *must* be carried out for this to be a great vintage (a great generation). Steps cannot be missed, even if they are painful for a time. For us to be part of the new wine of the Holy Spirit, we must be willing to go through our *crush time*, to allow the Spirit of God to remove all the stuff from us that would cause this wine to be bitter. The world needs a fresh drink, and we are it.

How can we be poured out as new wine if we are not first crushed, and then aged in a dark place to make the wine ready? The truths of God must be ingrained in us (fermented) so that they come out sweet and ready to be consumed.

Remember now, the process is to become all we are created to be and not to allow anything to remain that will spoil the end result.

THE PRESS OF GOD

Word: Lord God, Let Your glory come and cover all the earth. Your glory is as the water that covered the whole earth in the time of Noah. I believe this is a picture of Your Spirit. You have sent it out to cover the earth, yet there are still many who refuse to come under it. Let the water of Your Spirit come, Lord. Wash us away. Wash the "I" in us away Lord. Cover us in the sweet water (wine) of your Spirit.

Where are the strongholds in your life? In the mind. If you don't get involved in the pulling down of the strongholds of the flesh, then you will be endlessly set adrift with doubt and confusion. I can see us being swept along by the water of Your Spirit, riding along on the top but never getting in, never getting wet, soaked in Your love. We are eye to eye with those who are in the water, and we are missing it.

Marlene said that the Lord spoke to her during the service one morning, saying to her that Moses and I had much in common. I, too, was once young, handsome, and filled with zeal for the people of God. We also tried it our way and saw that it wasn't very fruitful. We, too, were taken to a desert place and prepared for what He really called us for (the apostle Paul had much the same experience).

Now He has called us back (as with the vision of the sheep) to help bring the Church out of bondage and to help it become the vital, powerful people of God that will become the true army of God in these last days. There was much dying to self in this process. Many times being uprooted to follow the cloud. Many lessons about learning to trust His leading. Abortive starts, false roads, missed directions, and the dark night of the soul. All of these were important parts of the maturing (pressing) we had go through. It's such a long process, yet goes by so quickly!

As I look back, it seems like just last week when I lived in Southern California, when in fact it has been more than 10 years ago. Truly, life is so short. It screams past you like a jet plane as you are standing still. I still think about the time when we went out to pastor our first church in 1978. In reality it was more than twenty-six years ago, and it could have been last year. Oh, how much He has done in such a short time. A wisp of smoke, a vanishing vapor, which is all this life is. The older you get, the easier it is to see. The Lord showed me a simple truth: The older I become, the less I remember and the more I know. If we allow,

He will winnow the yesterdays, which are no longer important for our tomorrows.

WHY?

Why salvation? Why did He save us? The Word of God says that God wants to restore us to a relationship with Himself so we can live with Him like we did before the fall of man. No walls, no obstacles, just relationship.

> *"But do not forget this one thing, dear friends: With the Lord a day is like a thousand years, and a thousand years are like a day. The Lord is not slow in keeping His promise, as some understand slowness. He is patient with you, not wanting* **anyone** *to perish, but everyone to come to repentance"* (2 Peter 3:8-9 emphasis added).

> *"For if, when we were God's enemies, we were reconciled to Him through the death of His Son, how much more, having been reconciled, shall we be saved through his life! Not only is this so, but we also rejoice in God through our Lord Jesus Christ, through whom we have now received reconciliation"* (Romans 5:10-11).

> *"All this is from God, who reconciled us to Himself through Christ and gave us the* **ministry of reconciliation**: *that God was reconciling the world to Himself in Christ, not counting men's sins against them. And He has committed to us the message*

of reconciliation. We are therefore Christ's ambassadors, as though God were making His appeal through us. We implore you on Christ's behalf: Be reconciled to God" (2 Corinthians 5:18-20 emphasis added).

Please see this with me. Christ Jesus, through Paul, is crying out to us how much He wants us to be rightly related with Him and then to take that relationship and model it for everyone we come in contact with. This is our ministry and our privilege and should be our joy. This is the same message that John is writing about in First John 1:4 when he says: *"We write this to make our joy complete."*

GOING BACK IS NOT AN OPTION

The following poem is my expression of Philippians 3:14-15:

There is no place to go but forward.

Going back is not an option;

yet, Lord, sometimes the way is not clear.

It's as if we have been going through a very thick forest.

Vines, trees, and bushes of all kinds block our vision; and yet,

going back is not an option.

Lead on, Lord, and we will follow You.

And if we must cut through with the sword

that which tries to hide the path, we will;

for going back is not an option.

If all we can do is go forward in the Spirit, we will.

If the only prayers we can pray are in the Spirit, we will;

for going back is not an option.

Thank you Lord for the sword of the Spirit to cut through all that which tries to entangle us and block our way.

Let's talk about the issues of holiness and righteousness! Two words come immediately to mind: Positional and Practical.

Positional: We are righteous because He is righteous.

Practical: Romans 6 says that righteousness comes by obedience. We must practice what God has given us. Righteousness is an "I am" and an "I do." We are to *do* the works of righteousness (see Rom. 6:17). Because we obey the teaching of Christ Jesus we are set free from sin and have become *slaves of righteousness.*

Obedience is not forced or legalistic, but willing. Paul calls it wholeheartedness! Wholehearted living, wholehearted being, which brings about wholehearted doing! We cannot live up to our potential without living a life of obedience. Reading James 1:19-22 and James 2:14-26 reveals what I mean. No! We are not saved by works. Salvation does not come through what you do. We are saved by faith, and that in Christ Jesus. *However, real faith produces real action!*

It's kind of like planting a fig tree that bears no fruit. It's useless. It's only an ornament. It's a tease, a false promise of things to come that never do. This is what Jesus was dealing with in Matthew and Mark when He cursed the fig tree. I hear Him telling His disciples to see the lack of fruit that exists in the religion of their day and that He is going to cause the tree to die so no one will ever expect to eat of it again. This is not unlike when Jesus told His followers to *"guard your hearts against the yeast of the Pharisees."* It's like the Church of today, empty, religion—religious Christianity. It promises so much but it is impotent. It has little or no power. The Church of Jesus' time was very different. Paul says, *"My message and my preaching were not with wise and persuasive words, but with a demonstration of the Spirit's power, so that your faith might not rest on men's wisdom, but on God's power"* (1 Cor. 2:4-5). And *"For the Kingdom of God is not a matter of talk but of power"* (1 Cor. 4:20). Without the manifested power of God in our midst, nothing changes. There's no fruit. It sounds good, but it's empty.

Today the spirit of intellectualism, which comes from eating of the tree of the knowledge of good and evil rather than the tree of life, has greatly infiltrated the Church. We are caught up in information and not revelation. Information is good, but unless it becomes revelation to our spirit, it only causes us to work, but doesn't change us into His image and likeness. Don't forget the former, but pray for the latter.

Power comes by being plugged into the real source of power, the Spirit of God, the Holy Spirit—not from information. The Holy Spirit is the holy power switch. It's His power working though us.

The real vine is Christ Jesus. Religion is a false vine. The real God, the living God, is the true vine. Somehow we have to come to the understanding that the power of God was always manifested when the Word of God was spoken. We, the Church, have settled for half the truth, and that is what most people preach. Why? Because it's not messy and it is safe. It's not the Three in One that is being taught. It's the "two and one." Understand that wherever the whole Gospel is not preached, a veil comes over the eyes of the hearer. The true Gospel lifts the veil and takes us into true relationship in the presence of God. (See Galatians 1:6-12; 2 Corinthians 4:1-6). We have left out the manifestation of the Holy Spirit, because He won't let us control the way that He interacts with His church. We want it to look like we think it should look and sound the way we believe it should sound. We are afraid that freeing the Spirit in our midst will mess up our church—our religious Christianity.

Again, I see us as being under the curse of the fig tree. Not literally, but we are not going to see what the real Church can be until we are honestly ready to give the management of it over to the Spirit of God. The Bible talks about having a form of godliness but denying the power within (see 2 Timothy 3:1-5). Therefore, what is the benefit of being slaves to God? The benefit is that it leads to holiness and the result of this is eternal life in Christ Jesus our Lord.

Word: Come on, come on, come on, rise up, oh, Church! How good does it have to get before you get excited about Jesus? About salvation? About life? Cry out for those who don't know the Lord. Cry out for those who are desperate for His help. Both the saved and the unsaved. Break off those chains that keep you in your seat as a spectator. Jump up and sing, for the God of all creation loves you and wants to visit you right where you are.

A funny thing is happening. The more I write to you about getting closer to the Lord, the more I know that I need to, as well. Take another step, Duane. I need the sweet refreshing of Your Spirit, Lord. Come, Lord, and rest on me and all those who are reading this book. Let the presence of Your Holy Spirit come and bring Your power to heal and set free all those who find themselves in the bondage of that which is false and is by some called truth.

He wants to release His divine power to flow through your life (see 2 Peter 1:4). This is the way it works now. His power through you! You are now the vessels that bring the promises to those in need. When Jesus was here, He did it. Now you are Sons and Daughters of God, and it is now your hands and mouths that the Holy Spirit works through. This is a joy and an honor to be chosen by the living God to carry on the work of restoration. Don't fear that people won't be healed. That's not your responsibility. Ours is to go. His is to heal and set free. It's not the mail-carriers' responsibility for what goes through the mail. Their only responsibly is to see that it gets delivered. God prepares the mail; we just deliver it. If you are in this ministry for yourself, you are going to be faced with hardships over and over in your life, until you come to the understanding that it is not about you, but it is all about Him. It's to His glory when someone is healed.

ALL ABOUT HIM—NOT ME

If you are still looking to Jesus for what He can do for you (all the promises of God), how He uses you, and what can you get from Him, you are still more of a baby Christian than a *new believer*.

God causes us to make choices. As new believers our focus is on us. What Jesus has done in our life, and what He does through us. "Oh, did you see how God used me to speak a word, or give a tongue, or to lay hands on so and so?" It's great to be used by God. It is really exciting and it builds up our faith. However, we must allow the Lord to change our focus from what He does through us to how we can serve Him and allow Him to come forth in and through us. A vessel for God is a vessel for God! Understand that God loves to bless His children, not because of what we do, but because of whose we are. This will go a long way in the maturing process.

How can I say this so it makes an imprint on our minds? People flocked around Jesus and followed Him everywhere He went. Why? Because of the miracles that He did. They wanted to see the power He had over sickness and disease, and of course, they wanted that power used on them. But there came a time when Jesus said "Enough! Now that you have seen the power, it is time for you to know who I am and follow Me for that and not for what I can do for you. I am the Bread of Life who has come down from Heaven. You must eat of My flesh and drink My blood to be my followers." (See John 6:53.) See also verse 66 which tells it like it is. *"From that time many of His disciples walked with Him no more."* (NKJV) In their hearts it was still all about them and what they wanted.

First Corinthians 3:1-4 and Hebrews 5:11-14 make the same point. Salvation is the cake, and what God does in us and through us is the frosting, or you might say the meat and the milk.

Those people in the Church who cannot get past what God does or does not do in their lives are stuck. Blessed and angry! Blessed when He blesses them and angry when He doesn't. This is all about self, and those who live this way can expect to be faced with difficult decisions (and choices) until they understand that it is all about God and what He wants and wills—not about them. These lessons are not easy to learn and live, nor is the process always quick; but I pray that you learn these lessons much more quickly than I did.

Please do not hear that we are not supposed to pray for our needs or ourselves. But hear that we must stop being self-absorbed. The tree of knowledge turns us into self-centered people from the God-centered people we need to be. Ask Him: How can this vessel be used by you, Lord, to help build up, edify, encourage, and strengthen the Body of Christ? If you had to choose someone to represent you as your ambassador to the rest of the world, would you choose someone who was weak and filled with doubt? No, probably not. You would most likely choose the very best person you could find. This is what God has done with you. You have been created to represent the living God, and as you yield to Him, He is conforming you to His image and likeness. The Bible says that the Spirit of God searches throughout the earth looking for hearts that are turned to God.

Word: I fill hungry souls. Are you hungry? Are you really hungry? If you are saying yes, it will be yes when the music is no longer playing. Do you hunger when you're alone? I will give My Spirit to those who hunger and thirst for Me.

JUST THOUGHTS

As I awoke on a Sunday morning to the first snow of the year, I was immediately filled with the wonderful understanding of the awesome, covering glory of Your blood. It covers everything. You can no longer see the debris in our lives, and all you can see is Your beauty, which has silently come down and covered us with a blanket of righteousness. Truly we are covered with a righteousness, which causes us to be white, as soft and as full of wonder as the fresh fallen snow.

Coming home from church, the snow was melting, and again I could see the debris fields emerging. I heard the Lord say to pray for His mercy to come and cover the piles of trash in people's lives.

Ask for His mercy, instead of His wrath (see Isaiah 1:18).

What Is God Speaking to Me?

_____

_____

_____

_____

_____

_____

_____

_____

_____

_____

_____

_____

_____

_____

_____

CHAPTER 13

THE RESTORATION OF ALL THINGS

(My Favorite Part)

"Who has blessed us in the heavenly realms with every spiritual blessing in Christ" (Eph. 1:3).

"HIS *divine power has given us everything we need for life and godliness..."* (2 Peter 1:3). This relates to the loss of all things in the garden (see Gen. 3:13-24). Here we have lost all the blessings, and we are driven out of the Garden of Eden and the presence of God.

In First Corinthians 15:45-46, we see a principle of God. First comes the natural and then comes the spiritual. Let me show you a picture of this from the Old Testament.

Did you know that the Old Testament, yes that's right, the Bible, is full of pictures? OK, so they're not photos, but they are pictures just the same. Word pictures of what God was doing, what He is doing, and what He is about to do. The Old Testament is the picture and the New Testament is the outline. Then again maybe it's just me. I see in pictures. When I read stories, like most of you, I visualize what is being said. Well, when I read the Bible, it comes alive, and I see it played out in front of me in my mind.

An example of what I mean: Read Second Samuel 9:1-13. These are only 13 verses in the Bible, yet if you see what I see, it will change your life. The story of David and Mephibosheth actually starts with the story of David (the boy who killed Goliath and later became king) and Jonathan (the son of King Saul). When Saul was planning to kill David, Jonathan, who was David's friend, warned him about his father's plan. David and Jonathan had made a covenant with each other (see 1 Sam. 19-20). After Saul and Jonathan had been killed, and David had taken his place as king, he remembered his promise to Jonathan.

In the day of kings, it was normal for the new king to kill off all the heirs of the previous king, so there would be no challenges to the throne. After the death of Jonathan and Saul, when David became king, one of Jonathan's servants took Mephibosheth, son of Jonathan and grandson of King Saul, and ran off to save him from being killed. During the escape, the servant dropped him. Both of his legs were damaged and he became crippled in both feet.

Years later David asked if there were any of Saul's relatives left who were still alive. Ziba, one of Saul's servants, told David that there was still a son of Jonathan alive and that he lived in Lo Debar. This was a town deep in Gileadite territory in Transjordan. As I understand, it was, as we might say, "across the tracks." Not a good place to live but a place that was relatively safe from David's rule. David sent for Mephibosheth and he was brought before the king. I can imagine that as Mephibosheth stood before King David, he expected to be put to death. And I believe that his response to David shows us what he believed his life was worth. "What is your servant that you should notice a dead dog like me"? He was convinced that his life was worthless. Second Samuel 9:8 proves it so.

But David remembers his promise to Jonathan and does the unexpected—he restores to Mephibosheth all that belonged to his father and gives him servants to do all the work. David then tells Mephibosheth that from now on, he will eat at the king's table for the rest of his life and still have the benefits of ownership of all of the inheritance, which he had lost. Hopefully, you are way ahead of me and can see the truths that I believe God has left here for us.

OUR STORY

Way back in the garden, you and I had lost everything because of man's sin. We were banished from the Kingdom of God and had to live in places we could find that were safe from the King. In Jeremiah 31:31-34, God makes the same type of covenant with us as David and Jonathan had made together. Again, we get to see the principle of first the natural and then the spiritual. God has grace for mankind and does the unexpected and restores all that we lost with the fall of man. This is why Ephesians 1 means so much to me. We have been given every spiritual blessing in Christ. Every one? Every one! How many? Every one!

From the beginning, man was to live forever. God's creation was perfect, and immortality was ours, but sin stole immortality from us, and now we live a mere mortal existence. God created us as close to Himself as humanly possible. *"And we, who with unveiled faces all reflect the Lord's glory, are being transformed into His likeness with ever-increasing glory, which comes from the Lord, who is the Spirit"* (2 Corinthians 3:18). Romans 8:29 says that we are *"conformed to the likeness of His Son."*

We as Christians have been living in a *subterranean* understanding of who God created us to be. We are living thousands of feet below the surface of understanding of who we are, buried beneath millions of tons of lies and vague teachings of our identities. The Holy Spirit has been drilling shafts for air and light to us to bring revelation so we can receive from God our true identity and allow Him to bring the truth and us to the surface once again. Immortality is ours once again, but this time it is found in our faith in Christ Jesus.

I can see it. Can you? Picture a rail car full of gold miners or coal miners resurfacing after a long shift of working underground, thousands of feet beneath the surface with the only light coming from a flashlight hooked to the front of the miners' helmets. Now for the first time in many hours, they come into the natural light of the sun. Relief and joy spread across their faces, and they can take huge breaths of fresh air. See yourselves as being freed right now from the bondage of not understanding who you were created to be. Let the light and breath of the Holy Spirit flow across you with that fresh revelation.

One morning as I was praying with one of our church's men's prayer groups, a pastor friend of mine felt like he needed to bring balance to what I was sharing because of some young believers who were there. Later in the day, I called him and what he said to me was *both shocking and expected*. He said, "You are pushing the envelope to its limit." He did add "where it should be," but it hit me like a religious bomb.

"Pushing the envelope" is an aeronautical term. I'm sure it is used in many ways, but as I understand it, it means operating at the outer safe limits of the design specifications for a certain type of aircraft. The designer and engineers set what they consider a safe operating envelope for their designed aircraft. Operating outside of this is unsafe and inviting failure of certain critical components, which we know can be disastrous.

Pushing the envelope of our Christianity creates more risk and yet can be much more rewarding. You are on the cutting edge of technology, the edge of understanding, seeing the impossible unfold before your very eyes. It is where Christianity began, and where I personally believe it is supposed to operate. God continues to reveal more of Himself and His plan and more of who we were created to be in Him. Do we deny this or do we go with it? I don't know about you, but I want to be caught living on the edge of Christianity, never going outside the lines (the Word of God), but always willing to obey the voice of God no matter how it may stretch me or my views.

I will always try to escape any box that people put me in. I want a fresh paradigm to live in and to see my God through. I won't ignore the many Scriptures that tell me He is bigger than I can comprehend and that His love is boundless.

John Wimber was a forerunner of his time—back in the 1980s, he was speaking on new paradigms. And recently I heard Dutch Sheets speak on paradigms and paradigm shifts. Again I say—get us out of the box. Even advertisers have taken hold of the concept. An advertisement for a Mexican food chain now calls for people to "think outside the bun."

Who does the Bible say will watch over His Word? See both Jeremiah 1:12 and Isaiah 55:8-11. Is it not the Holy Spirit's responsibility to lead us into all truth? We as Christians and Christian leaders continue to fall short of telling the whole truth for fear that someone will hear it and run wild. We just don't seem to understand that God wants that responsibility.

John G. Lake is one who understood more of his *identity in Christ* than most, and that was 80-100 years ago, and we (the Church at large) still don't get it. Lake said that God created man just a little lower than the angels, and He made us to reflect His image and likeness (see Ps. 8). History says that even the government understood that Lake was different and they called Spokane, Washington the healthiest city in the United States to live in, having 100,000 confirmed healings.

The truth is the truth, but the Church lives in fear that someone may abuse it. So let's water it down, or better yet, let's just ignore it. Oh, please don't hear what I am *not* saying. We are no longer perfect, and we have sin to thank for that. And we know that we can do nothing in ourselves without Christ. But my point is that we do have Him, and as the Bible story tells us, we have been restored and given back all things that were lost. Now tie this concept to First Samuel 30:18-25. Again the enemy steals everything that belonged to David and his men. You must read this to understand it. All was lost. But wait, God does not like that ending, and so He returns it all plus much more, and not just for the warriors, but for everyone.

P.S. MEPHIBOSHETH

One more interesting insight in the story of Mephibosheth. Because he was to have his feet under David's table, Mephibosheth's crippled condition would never show again; it was covered by the king's grace.

Isn't this like what the Lord does in our lives when we come to His table? All of our garbage is hidden under the robe. When the prodigal son returned, the first thing the father did was to put the family robe on him. Of course, this for us is the robe of righteousness. God has given us this beautiful picture of His love and mercy for us, and His faithfulness to His covenant.

It's very important to understand what God the Father did for God the Son. *"For God was pleased to have all His fullness dwell in Him, and through Him to reconcile to Himself all things, whether things on earth or things in heaven, by making peace through his blood, shed on the cross"* (Col. 1:19-20).

The following is one of the most important verses in the Bible pertaining to the believer. Oh! This is by far one of my favorites: *"Giving thanks to the Father, who has qualified you to share in the inheritance of the saints in the Kingdom of light"* (Col. 1:12). Did you notice that you did not qualify yourselves for this? God has given us the right to live in His Kingdom!

I think back on the old movies about kings and their kingdoms. I always picture the castle with a drawbridge coming down. Then the knights ride out of the castle, across the bridge, and into the green fields that separate the castle and the village. They charge hard on their horses, closing the distance quickly and into the center of town they come. There on a pole they nail the articles one must live by if they choose to live in this kingdom and come under the protection of the king and his armies.

The King of kings has a Book full of these articles. Have you read it? It's called the Bible! Obey what it says, and you, too, will be covered with His protection, but this time it's for all eternity.

We have been given a guarantee of this inheritance (see Eph. 1:13-14).

WHAT INHERITANCE?

Everything that belongs to Jesus has been given to us also. We are co-heirs with Him. (See Rom. 8:17.)

The story of the prodigal son is in reality the story of us. Except we are the other son—the one who stayed home, the one who had no idea what was his as a co-inheritor of his father's belongings. We must see ourselves as Romans 8:16 says, "*The Spirit Himself testifies with our spirit that we are God's children.*" What is so exciting about this is that it comes from His perspective and not from ours.

We, like Mephibosheth, will eat at the King's table, but we will eat there eternally, and the blood of Christ will cover our disgrace forever.

Throughout the years and all the changes and all of our questioning of God about His plans for Marlene and me, He has been speaking to us, slowly at first and now more and more. During that time one theme keeps returning to our minds—Adullam's cave revealed in First Samuel 22:1.

What Is God Speaking to Me?

_____

_____

_____

_____

_____

_____

_____

_____

_____

_____

_____

_____

_____

CHAPTER 14

THE CAVE

(Change & Transition)

FOR many years, we have been involved in the restoration of leaders. At times, we have even felt guilty for not having a burning passion for the unsaved. But we have come to the understanding now that the burning passion God has placed in our hearts is for lost leaders or those called to leadership. People hungry for the things of God but tired of religion and wounded by the Church or just by life in general. Those saints who have burned out or burned up for whatever the reason. They were on fire for Jesus and willing to do anything or go anywhere, and somewhere in the midst of the call of God, they began to receive those crippling blows, some from their own families, many from well-meaning brothers and sisters in the Body of Christ. These are the people we are called to help.

You can usually find them sitting in the back row of a larger church with arms folded, protecting themselves from everyone and everything. Or they may have simply dropped out and God causes you to meet them at work or while you are getting your nails done, as happened to Marlene. You are called by God to go into their cave and help them rediscover who they are in Christ. The purpose of the *Adullams Cave* experience is to prepare us for a new direction.

CHANGE

Many things must first take place for us to be ready for God to send us in a new direction. We must be cleansed of the old and ready for the new. This is not a delicate operation. As in the birthing process there is a time of transition without which the birth would be very dangerous and possibly result in death. The baby must be in the correct position for the birth to go well.

Many of us have grown used to our old ways of existing, and whether it's good or bad, it's where we are most comfortable. It can be destroying us, and still, if given the chance, we will return to it just like the Hebrews wanted to return to Egypt. Leeks anyone? (See 2 Peter 2:21-22). This is why God many times has to make the old ways very distasteful to us so that we don't want to stay there any longer. The truth is, the old ways may not even be bad ways of doing things; they are just no longer what God wants you to do.

EXAMPLE

We have been pastors for approximately 30 years. Those years have been broken up with times of traveling on the road, working with para-church organizations, and some times of just plain full-time work outside the Body of Christ. We see these times as opportunities for God to educate us, and prepare us for the next place He chooses for us to serve. We are waiting for what's next!

Why is it that so many of us believe we can change something in our lives without letting go of it? Many times, what is next is just out of reach, and no matter how much you stretch, you just can't quite get there. You must let go of the past to get to the future.

JOHN AND MARSHA'S STORY
(NAMES HAVE BEEN CHANGED)

My wife Marlene met Marsha one day while getting a manicure. They enjoyed the conversation and exchanged phone numbers. Marlene invited Marsha and John to our church, and a couple of Sundays later they showed up. We had lunch together and a bond began to form. We didn't know it at the time, but found out later that when they came to us, they were DOA—"dead on arrival," according to Marsha.

They had been part of the leadership of a church and had moved here to help plant a new work. Nine years later they were DOA and without hope. Marlene and I had the privilege of being the instruments God chose to breathe His life back into them. For almost six months, we poured everything we could think of into them. They were like baby birds in their nest when mom or dad shows up with dinner. We just couldn't fill them up fast enough. Their hearts were open like the mouths of the baby birds. They began to blossom, and life flowed from their lips once again. They devoured our videotape library. God had a plan for this couple and it was easy to recognize their true gift of encouragement. The more we shared with them, the more they encouraged us.

God is always doing more at one time than we understand. He was calling them to a new ministry somewhere else, and they needed restoration and refreshing before they left. Now they are being used by God to share that gift, and others that they possess, in another place. What a joy to hear from them and see what God is in the process of doing in and through them.

God has spoken to us that they are coming, people like John and Marsha, "prodigals," and we are to be prepared! We have been in prayer about this ministry off and on for a year or so, and we believe that now is the time to act.

Let me ask you two questions:

1. If God spoke to you in an audible voice and asked you to make a big change in your life, would you say yes to Him? Most of you would say "yes."

2. If you heard a very small voice inside telling you to make a small adjustment in your lifestyle, would you do it?

Those of you who answered yes to the second question are the ones who will be used by God to lead the army of warriors that He is preparing and making ready to bring into His Church.

God spoke the following word to me. "I am raising up an army of young warriors to fight in the next millennium. This was before the year 2000. But young warriors are not to lead, they are to fight."

God has seasoned leaders, mature saints that He has been preparing to lead this army. Some of them are obvious and some He has had put away, sequestered, stashed in places you wouldn't imagine. Many of us have spent time in one of these unimaginable places.

There are many different names for this place, which I call "the Cave." Here are a few other biblical names and the people associated with them:

1. Adullam's Cave (David)
2. The Wilderness (Jesus)
3. The Pit (Paul)
4. The Cistern (Joseph)
5. Prison (Joseph)
6. The Desert (Israel)
7. The Grave (Lazarus)
8. The Church (All of us)

THE CAVE OR HIDING PLACE

What does the "cave" stand for? I can think of no better term to relate the cave to than this: It has many of the same characteristics as the womb. I think you will see that this place has many characteristics you are familiar with. It's similar to the place where we were all formed and developed. What do we know about this place?

The womb is:

An environment that encourages growth and development.

A place of protection.

A place of nourishment.

A place of security.

A place of concealment.

A place from which one is birthed.

A private place of intimacy.

DAVID'S CAVE EXPERIENCE

Let's look to the early years of David's life and see what we can learn from his experience.

"...*I'll pin David to the wall...*" (1 Sam. 18:10-12). God had to begin the process of disillusionment in David about where he was and who he worked for. Think about it. Here he is working for the King, playing his harp to soothe the King's spirit. What a great job. In all of history, only a few are chosen for this type of call, and with all the benefits of the position, it would be very hard to make the decision on your own to leave, so the king does it for him and tries to pin him to a wall with his spear. Not just once but twice! He got the message. It is time to move on.

Is pride hiding in your heart? (see 1 Sam. 18:12-16). What lurks in the heart of man? Jer. 17:9 "*The heart is deceitful above all things and beyond cure.*"(1 Sam. 18:27-28). David attempts to impress his king and does twice what has been asked of him. But instead of finding favor, he finds that he has helped make the King jealous of him (see 1 Sam. 19:9-10). Now David has to flee for his life from the King.

This process is called "dying to self" or "dying to your dreams." Now God starts pruning (in the natural the farmer calls on neighbors to help prune his vines because they must be cut way back to produce a good crop the next season). This can also be called the stripping process. In woodworking (restoration) it is doing all the preparation, such as stripping, sanding, even re-warping, whatever it takes to restore it to new condition, or at least to the way you want to use it.

David:

(a) loses his job and has to run for his life. God strips away all the things he is used to having.

(b) is no longer in his leadership role. He lost his job, no more money.

(c) loses his wife. (See 1 Samuel 18:20-22; 19:11-17.)

(d) no longer has a mentor to look to for guidance. (See 1 Samuel 19:18-24.)

(e) loses his best friend. (See 1 Samuel 20:1-3,42.)

(f) even loses his self-respect. (See 1 Samuel 21:10-13.)

Although David hides away, look who comes to be with him in the cave (see 1 Samuel 22:1).

His family! And they don't even like him. They're jealous of him. He's the baby brother and they make him their meal ticket. Those in debt; those in distress; those who are discontented. (See 1 Samuel 22:2.)

Are you feeling under pressure? Can't pay those pesky bills? Do you feel wronged? People just don't understand you? Have your friends turned against you? Have you been mistreated? Well, welcome to the cave. Come on into the joy of experiencing fellowship with those who, like you, have arrived at the same location—under a dark cloud!

DESPERATION!

Please read Psalm 142:1-7 and Psalm 57:1-7 to see the desperation with which David is crying out. You can see from these verses that this was not an easy time for him!

God certainly is a God of challenge, isn't He? But He does have a plan.

The cave is not the beginning or the end; it's only a stopping off place. It's a place of restoration, refreshment, and a good place to be taught. It's a place He seems to send us before He gives us a new direction, a new lease on life for you and for all those He sovereignly brings to you.

A NEW FOCUS

In the cave you may hear God say something like: You are to become my discipler! These people will become a mighty army for Me, and you are going to lead them. I'm giving you a new focus, a new job, a new mentor, a new best friend. This will be bigger than you could ever imagine. You will no longer have to hide from Saul or run for your life. (See Isaiah 43:18-19 and Psalm 34.)

WHY THE CAVE?

To give new life and new meaning to those I bring you. To restore personal dignity and direction. To help them understand who they are, and who I have called them to be. To restore leaders to the front lines.

David was not prepared for his calling. At the time of his anointing, all he was prepared for was shepherding and fighting and harp playing. God was going to cause him to go to a new level. He had no idea how to be a King.

Someone has said, "gifting can take you places where lack of character won't keep you." Gifting and character are not the same. David had potential, but it was not developed.

VISION

Most Christians are rather like undeveloped film negatives. While I was on my way to the store to have some film developed, the Lord showed me a picture of what most Christians are like and how they resemble the film I was taking in. As is, film is just a roll of hope that could hold great promise. As it goes through the first process, there is a shadow that appears to show the promise of a beautiful picture. However, it takes the full process of development for us to see the real picture. Without development, it is only an unfulfilled promise of what is available—of what might be. You and I were born as packages of promise, and with the right care and development, we turn out as negatives that show a shadow of what we can be in Christ. As we give ourselves to Him, more and more of the darkness disappears, and the true purpose of our birth comes into focus.

God was developing David and preparing him for his future.

TEACH AND ALLOW

Pastors and teachers must learn to "teach and release." By release, I mean allow people to "become" all that God created them to be.

As pastors or mature believers, we have the tendency to teach to conform. Teach and correct. But we are called by God to correct sin, not immaturity. We teach and God conforms! Traditionally, we have had this wrong. From the time of the Pharisees until now, we have tried to conform people into what we believed was best for them. I think we believe that God has released this responsibility to us, but I for one do not share in this belief system—religious Christianity—any longer.

If we teach the Word of God and allow God a free hand in people's lives, then I believe they will become the gifts that He had in mind for them to be in the Body of Christ. We are all guilty of using our own hammer and chisel to shape people (to knock off all those things that we deem unsightly) into these beautiful works of art that have *our* resemblance, but they have never been fully developed by the conforming work of the Holy Spirit. We try to save people from all the pitfalls that we went through. I see the word "conforming" (with the root word *form* as in Genesis 2:7) similar to what a potter does to the clay he puts on the wheel. See also Romans 9:21.

PREPARATION: GOD'S WINNOWING PROCESS

What are some of the special abilities that David needed for his calling?

1. To have the heart of a warrior.
2. To know how to be an authority figure.
3. To know how to hear from God and then to wait on His timing.
4. To know the importance of the people God brings into his life.

What needs to be ready for this change? (See Proverbs 3:3,4.)

1. Obedience comes first then (John 13)
2. Humility, which leads to
3. Trust in God, which causes (John 13).
4. Identity, which builds
5. Long suffering, which takes
6. Faithfulness, which develops
7. Leadership, which opens (John 13)
8. Servanthood, which you must have to
9. Lead, as God modeled for us in Jesus.

There was much to learn for David, and the cave was the perfect environment.

CHARACTER TRAITS

Obedience is being subject to authority, willing to obey. (See Proverbs 3:5-6.) The middle part of *obe<u>die</u>nce* is what? die!

Obedience first starts with family. Doing the small stuff. David had to do the work of a shepherd while his brothers went off to war. The mundane work with an occasional exciting moment—killing a lion and a bear to protect the sheep, provided very useful bits of training for what was ahead for him. Killing Goliath the giant was one of the greatest feats using this training, as well as defeating the other giants he faced in his lifetime.

Second, after the anointing by Samuel to be king, David did not try to make it happen, but waited for God's timing.

Third, do what is in front of you to do. It's all part of the training. Don't try to skip ahead or take a shortcut.

Using David as an example of cave preparation, we must move up from here, take a step up to a higher place if we want it all. That's all part of what God has planned for your life. His vision for you is so much larger than yours. A new beginning awaits us with the fresh understanding of what we have gleaned from our cave experience.

What Is God Speaking to Me?

_____

_____

CHAPTER 15

WE ARE THE
TEMPLE OF GOD

(Radical Christianity Cannot Live in Buildings)

I include this vision here because it has to do with true restoration:

One day I was sitting on my sofa listening to worship and I began to see a vision. At first, I could not see it clearly because it was very dark, but then there appeared a very small bit of light coming from around what looked like rubble. This all happened as if it were part of a movie. Then a little more light came in, and I could see more clearly. It looked like the Temple Mount, but it was just rocks and they were spread over the ground. Then all of a sudden, miraculously the rocks began to move, and the temple started to be reconstructed. It was coming together, but not by the hands of man. Supernaturally, the Temple came together. As this took place, the light began to get brighter and brighter.

Again, it's like in a movie, and the camera spans wider and now I could see what was really taking place.

The Temple has come together and is now complete except for the roof. I was now looking down and I could see the outer court, the inner court, and the Holy of Holies. More light appeared and the camera pulled back once more. Wow! As I looked, I saw that the Temple had been reconstructed in the torso of a man. He is transparent and lying on the ground, and the Temple filled his body from the waist to his neck. At this point, the Lord spoke to me saying: "*You are the Temple of God!*" You, just like the Temple, have an outer court (flesh), you have an inner court (soul), and you have a Holy of Holies (spirit). As this was being said, the camera seemed to span wider once again and I could see more of the picture. More light shone and the camera's view opened completely and I saw what I thought was the entire picture.

The man appeared to be waking up. As he does, he stretches out his arms, he hits and knocks loose the mosque on the Temple Mount. The mosque begins to roll along his arms and behind his neck and over to the other arm. It reminded me of what some basketball players can do with the ball when they're just playing around. Then it came back and over to the other arm, and just as I thought it was going to fly off the end of his hand, he wrapped his hand over it and drew it back into his chest, which is where the Holy of Holies is.

I had trouble understanding this vision at first, but then the Lord said to me: "I died for all men, and these who are represented by the mosques are also made in my image and likeness." (Since the terrorist attack in the United States on September 11, 2001, this word has taken on even more meaning to me.) Then the man began to sit up, and the camera drew back once more.

He stood up and began to walk. Up to this point, the entire vision was in black and white except for the dome on the mosque, which was gold. As he took each step, as his heels rose up, I could see beautiful green grass and flowers blooming in brilliant colors. God spoke to me again and said that when mankind understands who I have created them to be they will take life *everywhere* he puts his feet!

What this is communicating to us is: (1) God is restoring His temple in our time so that His presence can again dwell among us, and (2) we were all created by design. There is a plan to our creation. No, not just a plan, more than that—a pattern. We were created in the image and likeness of God. I realize that this is not new news to you, but hear me out.

THE PURPOSE OF THE TABERNACLE (EXODUS 26)

God puts Himself in our midst. The Temple gives us a physical manifestation of the Three and One. The Temple is tangible, something that can be experienced, and something that can be seen and shared by everyone. God spoke to Moses and gave him the exact plans for the Temple which was also a representation of Himself and then told him to build it. It was a Tabernacle in the wilderness which had an outer court, an inner court, and a Holy of Holies. Three and One—a picture or type of God Himself. Then He had Moses cover it with skin. Dyed red skins of the ram—a picture of Jesus and His blood on the Cross. Then a covering of badger skins, some Bible translations use "sea cows"—a picture or type of you and me. You and I are now the Temple of God. This body covered with skin now holds the Ark of the

Covenant. Right here inside us! We are the Temple, and this is where the presence of God lives.

After giving Moses instructions about how to build the Ark of the Covenant, God told him what to place inside of it. "*Then put in the Ark the Testimony, which I will give you*" (Exod. 25:16). The Ten Commandments, Moses' rod that budded, and the jar of manna that He fed them with in the desert (see Exod. 16:33; Heb 9:4). Now let's tie this to Revelation 12:11, "*They overcame him...by the word of their testimony....*" What does this say to us today? God now writes the commandments on our hearts, and we are a living testimony. I see that Exodus 25:16 is for you and me today: "*Then put in the ark the Testimony, which I will give you.*" We have been called the Tent of God, or the Tent of Meeting. This is in the pattern of the original Tent of Meeting that God gave to Moses in the wilderness.

God is three parts, Father, Son, and Holy Spirit, and yet He is one God. We are three parts, spirit, soul, and body, and yet one person (see 1 Thess. 5:23). The Temple is three parts, the outer court, the inner court, and the Holy of Holies, and yet one Temple.

When we truly come into the understanding of who we really are and what the purpose of our existence is (see Romans 5:18, the ministry of reconciling lost man back to God), life will take place everywhere we go, and along with this will be the understanding that every person is precious in His sight. We are to pray for the whole of mankind, not just for the ones who are easy for us to understand.

When we ask Jesus Christ into our hearts to be Lord and Savior, a marvelous work takes place. The *Great Architect* is at work forming a new you. We become the Temple of God, designed after the pattern given by God, and each one of us has the same three parts as the original Temple—the Outer Court, the Inner Court, and the Most Holy Place.

I believe that each one of us must enter the Most Holy Place to have the relationship with God that Jesus paid for, wants, and prays for us to have as revealed in John 17.

How do we enter in? To me, it seems as if our soul is the veil which separates us from intimate relationship with the Father and that we must rend this veil on a daily basis. It's as if something up between the ears, some part of our soul, joins forces with the *seamstress from hell* to sow up the rip in the veil. There is a definite effort being made (a war is raging) to keep us separated from relationship with our God.

As the veil was torn when Jesus died on the Cross, we, too, must die to rip the veil in two and enter in. We must die to ourselves, die to our mind, will, and emotions. The flesh! We have to break through this veil again and again—every time the enemy of our souls tries to close it up. The cost for Him was everything. Now, how much are we willing to pay for relationship with Him? To gain all He has for us we must go beyond religious Christianity.

God had the Temple and Tabernacle built to house his blessings. After Jesus gave His life for us—we became the Temple and Tabernacle. Now we have to walk outside the buildings and into the world filled with people who need to hear the Good News of Jesus Christ.

True communion with the Father comes from the crushing of the flesh and the emptying of our lives. Jesus' cup was emptied on the Cross. His body went through a tremendous pressing in the garden, a crushing that brought pain and eventually death, which in reality brought life. You and I daily face the same opportunity to live for Christ and to die to self.

PATTERNS

Throughout the Bible there are patterns revealing God's orderly plans for all of His creation. The following are only a few that reflect our focus.

God created the earth and laws including gravity
(see Genesis).

God gave Moses the exact *pattern* of the sanctuary
(see Exod. 25:8-9).

God gave David the exact *pattern* of the Temple
(1 Chron. 28:11).

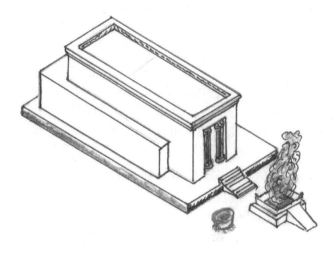

As we have seen in Thessalonians, we have three parts: spirit, soul, and body, and we are the Temple of God (see 1 Cor. 6:19).

The Temple has three parts: Holy of Holies, Inner Court, Outer Court.

God promises to give us a new heart in place of a heart of stone. (See Ezekiel 36:26.)

God plants His seed (sperma) in us.

We have the DNA of God in us. (See 1 John 3:9-10; 14:15; 15:15; 16:7.)

Also, the Sanctuary is a pattern of what is in Heaven (see Heb. 8:5), shadows of things to come (see Col. 2:17).

1. Pattern God: Father, Son, Holy Spirit who was, who is, who is to come.
2. Pattern Temple: Holy of Holies, Inter Court, Outer Court.
3. Pattern Man: spirit, soul, body.

THE PRESENCE OF GOD

The story of Obed-Edom as told in Second Samuel 6:9-12 is an absolutely amazing picture of how our God desires to bring His blessing on us as we sit in His presence. As the story goes, David had gone out, following the desires of his soul, to do a good thing and had not taken the time to discover just how God would take a *good* thing and turn it into a *God* thing. God had a plan, but David, in his desire to rush ahead, did it the way he believed it should be done. Can we relate?

Well, in our story, God was not to be handled by man, and the result was that David's plan was put on hold for some time while he worked out his upset and misunderstanding with God. In the meantime God was doing a God thing with the household of Obed-Edom. Because David got confused, he had the Ark taken to Obed-Edom's house for safekeeping, so guess what happened. Everything of Obed-Edom's was blessed. The awesome presence of God and His desire to bless His children was at work, and everything in the vicinity of the Ark had the blessing of God on it.

As David heard the news about this, I think it made him consider how he could bring the presence of God into the city so God's presence could bless his life and everyone's around him. Now he took the time to find out what the correct way was to move the Ark and to reap the blessing.

So often we want the presence or blessings of God, but we want it to happen the way we think it should, but our God has a plan which He has worked out for our good. He wants to bless us and has given us the way to this blessing, but we must take the time to find it.

Let's use this illustration: Suppose you are looking for gold, and you suspect that you have the right location. Now, how do you begin to mine it? If you rush in without the proper plan, you could be caught in a cave-in. The gold is there waiting for you. Do you rush in and take a chance of failing? Or do you discover how to shore up as you go, and then safely and surely discover all the blessings that await you? Let's take the time and discover God's way to blessing.

A good way to start is to look at Jesus as our *pattern* (see Matt. 6:9-15) *"on earth as it is in heaven."* This is key to understanding.

Why? God prayed it! Jesus, God the Son, is showing and leading us to discover the true gold field.

We are not just family by faith, but we are family by blood. When we call Him Father, we are right, because He put His seed, His sperm, His life in us (1 John 3:9). As God called Abraham the Father of many nations, we can view this as a pattern from Heaven of what He has done for those who have asked Him to come into their hearts.

The key to understanding who we are and who we are designed to be: Created in His image and likeness—created by design. The pattern remains. God is the same, yesterday, today, and forever!

COLORING WITHIN THE LINES

We are the Body of Christ with many members and gifts (see 1 Cor. 12).

As we all learned to color inside the lines in our coloring books that had pictures already drawn for us, God has given us the pattern that we as individual Christians must work within to rightly reflect our Lord.

I will share an illustration from my own life. As a hair stylist in a very exclusive salon, I was involved in many styling shows. Different coiffeur guilds in the Southern California area would sponsor hair styling competitions and invite stylists from all over to come and compete against one another. The guilds would give us the pattern weeks in advance, so we could create new and exciting styles within the framework they set forth. Instead of being restrictive as some may think, this challenged us to be very creative in our individual designing efforts.

The pattern would be something like this: height must not exceed 6" in the crown area, width will not be more than 2" on the sides and not more than 1" below the ear. From the crown, the length must taper to 0 at the nape line. The bang area will not exceed 2" in height. Now it was up to us to let all our creative skills come forth. We would use multiple colors to flow from one area to the next to highlight the swirls and curls and to exaggerate the flow of the wave patterns.

Hopefully you get the idea. God has been crafting all of us and made all of us individuals who think and respond very uniquely in every situation we find ourselves in. He has given us freedom of expression to voice the love and mercy that He put within us, only we must stay within the pattern He gave us. That pattern is, of course, Jesus Christ. Knowing this allows us to develop many wonderful and uniquely different skills as ministers of His Gospel.

When our hairstyles were being judged, they would come by with rulers to inspect our work. Points would be taken off for each place we didn't stay within the prescribed pattern—within the lines. For many years, the Church has been busy coloring outside the lines in our "religious" effort to create a user-friendly church. I'm not sure how God will judge us, but it will most likely be along these lines. What have you done with My Son? How have you obeyed His Word? Did you do what He did? Did you say what He said?

Please read Matthew 6:9-15—The Lords' Prayer. *Thy kingdom come on earth as it is in heaven.* This is His "pattern." Not only was

He teaching us how to pray, but He was also showing us priority and giving us the pattern.

I have to tell you that I have preached this passage many times and have heard others teach this with great insight, and I still did not see this.

Now re-read Matthew 6:9-15. What jumps out at you? Daddy-Abba; giving glory to the Father; thanksgiving; reverence to God; God's rule on earth; tomorrow's bread today; forgiveness? Any or all of these are wonderful truths; that's pretty much what we have taught for years. But now let's ask the Lord what we are lacking in our understanding of this word. Let's think just for a minute about who it is teaching us how to pray. God the Son! Jesus. This is not Matthew speaking, or Paul or John, or any one of the disciples—it is the one and only true God, the God of all creation.

Ask yourself this question. Do you think that the One who spoke the world into existence, the One who hand-formed man and woman, the One who put light for day and a lesser light for night, might know what we need? Do you think that He might have a good idea what it is going to take for His Word to be walked out?

OK, exactly what is it that Jesus is communicating to us through this prayer? Let the Kingdom of God come, let the will of God reign, let the authority of God rule on the earth as it is in Heaven. Some say that this is yet to come, but Jesus is in the process of giving His followers practical advice for everyday living. Why would He throw in something for the future in the midst of everyday teaching? I don't believe that He is calling for us to not be people who use our will, because it is going to take our will to live out what He is saying. He is saying that He wants to use you—your spirit, soul, and body—to carry out His will on earth as it is in Heaven. Maybe you are asking yourself right now, how is this possible? Who are you? Who did He create you to be? His representative, His ambassadors, His hope to this world!

I would like to leave this chapter and start the next with a caution that the Lord gave me.

CAUTION! RUNNING AHEAD IS:

Dangerous,

Painful,

and can be Deadly!

What Is God Speaking to Me?

_____

_____

_____

_____

_____

_____

CHAPTER 16

RUNNING AHEAD CAN CAUSE GREAT PAIN

I had a very real dream: Marlene and I were in the front yard of my friend Jeff's house. Jeff was a childhood buddy, only now this dream took place in the present. Across the street was the real movie ranch, which at the time when I grew up was owned by Ralph McCutchens. This ranch had all the buckboards, stagecoaches, covered wagons, horses, and tack used in almost all the early Western movies. This was a real part of my boyhood adventures. I used to clean stalls and do odd jobs around the ranch just to be close to all the history and adventure that it represented to me. We could sit in a stagecoach and be transformed back in time while waiting for the bad guys to come and try to steal the gold box.

Out front there was a large corral where they used to hold rodeos and train the horses. In this dream, I saw one of our ex-pastors sitting on top of a semitrailer like a stagecoach driver, with a team of horses out in front and a big bullwhip with which he was driving them very hard around the corral. This held great significance for Marlene and me at the time, but it is not the point I want you to see. There was another friend in the yard with us. He was my closest friend and the worship leader in our church in Fort Bragg, California. His name is Warner and his wife's name is Pennie. They are a great couple and dear friends we have known for more than 25 years.

Well, in this dream, Warner decided to get into his car and leave, and he wanted Marlene and me to follow him. We did, and once we were on the freeway, we were moving quite fast, and someone got between our cars. Warner made a sudden turnoff, and by the time I saw this I could not make that turnoff safely. At this point, I decided to take the next turnoff, go back, and see if he was waiting for us. When we turned off, we discovered to our shock that there was no way to go back from there.

I found myself driving down an alleyway with businesses on either side. I saw an electric supply store and I went in to ask directions. I was told that I would have to go all the way back to the beginning and start over to get back to the turnoff that we missed. It was the only way. Marlene and I left there very disappointed, and as we were walking along, we came to a space between the buildings where a store used to be, but it appeared to have burned down. As we stood looking at this, we could see that where we wanted to go was just on the other side of this lot, which was now only a broken foundation and debris. We knew that all we had to do was cross this lot and we could be back on track, so Marlene, not waiting for me to lead out, went through the fence and began to run ahead of me. Now, this was not easy for her because she was wearing a short skirt, high heels, and black hose (this is not a true picture of how she dresses).

There was a large pile of earth or rock in the way which was about 10 feet high, so she started to climb it. But she lost her footing and fell, tearing her hose. She began again to climb, and fell again, but this time I was there to catch her. After this she decided to follow me, and I found another way around this pile of rubble. We went around to the right, and there was just enough room between the broken foundation and the wall of the business next door for us to barely get past. As we went, we could see that the foundation was broken more or less in the center, where at one time, there must have been a basement. Both halves were caved in to the center, and now there was a pool of water there. People were playing in the pool, and there was a stream of water coming in from the front under the fence that blocked our way to the street where we wanted to go. As we made our way along the front of the property, it was very tight. We had to hold onto the fence and slowly, foot by foot, make our way through the small river of water to a fence on the other side of this lot. We finally made it, and I was able to help Marlene through and then get through myself. As we came out, the dream ended.

For me it was obvious that we were looking for direction, which we received and which we did not follow. Because of this, we were faced with many challenges, which were very real, as it turned out. Old foundations had to be broken to make a place for a river anointing. We went through it still looking for our way. We had a couple of very difficult setbacks that cost us a lot, both in time and resources. This dream turned out to be very prophetic. There is so much here that I cannot go into it all.

My point in telling you all of this is that running ahead, not listening to the counsel you have received, and looking for short cuts are not good things to do, and they are definitely not wisdom. My prayer is that you will take a tip from someone with gray hair: Don't do those things!

You are probably like most people who don't want to hear the "W" word. Yes, it stands for *wait*. Wait on the Lord, and don't jump before He gives you the direction and the release to go. This is not easy to hear or easy to do, but again, do what is in front of you to do, and it will save you time and pain.

RED LIGHT, GREEN LIGHT

One day while Marlene and I were in my delivery truck—I had a delivery route, and Marlene worked along with me—we were behind a woman who stopped at a traffic signal, but the light in front of her was green. However, there was another light just ahead and that one was red—the woman had her eyes on the red light instead of the green light nearest to her.

Marlene said to me that if you look too far ahead, you will stop, instead of doing what God has given you a green light for accomplishing.

Our walk is a day-by-day walk, and if we look too far forward, to the future light, then we can miss the very thing that God is asking us to do today. Things such as knowing the open doors that He put before you—killing the giant, working for the King. Be loyal to what God has given you to do. We must first do what is right in front of us and do it as unto God. He will open the right door at the right time.

Waiting on the Lord requires obedience. Obedience requires humility. The definition of humility is lowly, meek, not proud. Humility is a being not a doing (see John 13). You can't do humility; God must be allowed to do this work in you. This is where we learn to die to the things that hinder God working effectively through us. I believe that it is Joyce Meyer, Christian speaker and author, who calls this process *"A real flesh burner."*

God desires to pour us out as an offering just as He did His first son Jesus. First we need to: Die to self—die to *our* way of working it out.

Then we need to: Defer to Him—our ambitions, our plans, our goals, our rights, and our pride in the calling.

And finally: Understand that calling and gifting are *not* enough.

Taking these steps lead to: Trust in God—confidence, reliance, implicit faith in the plans He has for us.

God will give us ample opportunities to learn these lessons, without which we will most definitely crash and burn. These are so important to God that He will see to it that this class will remain "in session" our entire lives. The lessons never end. We do, however, learn to let the process build us up and not wear us down. A modern-day David might say: "Now wait just a darn minute here, God! You had me anointed as King, right? Why do I have to wait and be treated like this? Am I not the rightful leader of the people now? I'm the king! I. I. I. But Saul's not doing it right, Lord, so it must be the right timing for me to come forth, right, Lord? This waiting can't be of you, Lord. After all, people are being abused here. Lord, kings don't run, do they? Kings don't hide, do they?"

Can you imagine how David must have felt when he had the kingdom within his reach. "Now, Lord, this has to be the right time; you've placed him right into my hands. Right, Lord?" Attitude adjustment time (see 1 Sam. 24:3-22). I believe what the Lord wants us to see from this story is the difference between what our feelings tell us and what He wants us to do, or as in this case, to be. God was teaching David how to trust Him in all things and we need to pay attention to this also. Our flesh would tell us to kill this person who is after us, but God says, "I have a plan and you need to learn to do things My way if you want to truly be victorious."

IDENTITY CRISIS

Who am I? What's happening here? David is discovering his identity. What do I really believe?

First. We must learn all the right terms about what God has to say about us. We are kings and priests, more than conquerors in all things. Joint heirs with Christ, Children of God, we are even called greater than John the Baptist. "*The Lord will make you the head, not the tail. If you pay attention to the commands of the Lord your God that I give you this day and carefully follow them, you will always be at the top, never at the bottom*" (Deut. 28:13). Now, after becoming very comfortable with who we are, we have all the ammunition we need to go out and destroy the enemy, and everyone else who stands in our way!

Watch out leaders. Look behind you. Are people following you because you know how to serve them, or are they following you out of fear or for what you can do for them? Are they healthier now than when you first came into their lives to help them?

Look carefully and see if what you say and what you do (model) are really the same.

ɲust be found in Christ and who He is,
ɩ we can do for Him. This is works and

…at we join Him in crucifixion—like him, this
ɩes, any more then Jesus did.

ɔɩ careful, some of you will remain in the cave (a
ɑll of your lives, and you will believe that "life is
and that this is your lot, your cross to bear.

Some of you have been in the cave for so long that you don't
even know that you are in a cave. Years have gone by, and you
believe that this is just the way things are supposed to be. Why?
Because you won't give up and give in to the urging of the Holy
Spirit. You won't release the hurt, pain, disappointment, and dis-
illusion that brought you into the cave in the first place.

You are still angry with God and His way of doing things, and
you don't want to take the risk of re-establishing a correct relationship with Him or anyone else if there is a chance you might
get hurt again.

Let me illustrate.

Marlene and I were praying with a beautiful woman one day.
This woman experienced a horrendous teen life. She was held as
a prisoner in a cultic group and was raped repeatedly, used on a
daily basis, beaten and locked in an outside shed without clothes,
and with bugs and spiders crawling over her because she was
caught trying to escape. She was forced to witness the sacrifice
of her own puppy that the cult leaders had given to her and
allowed her to become very attached to. Then they sacrificed the
puppy and poured its blood over her. Other things happened that
are just too gross to share. Now 30 years later, after raising her

family she is reliving this terrible nightmare, and she is suffering from Post Traumatic Stress Syndrome.

She could not believe she was worth God healing her and became her own worst enemy. For years she looked good on the outside, raised her children, and dealt with life, but she had no idea of what was going on deep down on the inside of her. We have spent time trying to help her establish her true identity by helping her see herself as God sees her. At last report she is doing much better.

Word: We can dress to the max, look good, have our hair done, and our shoes shined, smell good, and still have garbage in our pockets. The ants are eating away at our identity without our knowledge.

There will come a time when God will reveal things to us, things that are killing us, and at that time, we must be willing to let him deal with it and heal this part of our life.

As with Lazarus, God did not tell him to remove his own grave clothes but has given us (you and me) the job of taking off the grave clothes for others. Be very careful here and know that it is God's timing and not yours—let Him give you the green light. Our job is to be a part of the solution for those God puts in our lives and not more of a problem. It has been said that "the larger the investment the greater the returns." Development is painful, it costs time, it involves risk taking, determination, and hard work, and this you have to do for yourself. It can't be done for you. Many of you have dreams and visions, but fear has stopped you from going on. God has done all the groundwork and given you all those wonderful promises, but now it's your turn. You have to receive, and sometimes *this is not easy*.

If we are the vessel, and what God does in our lives is the fruit that is being crushed and made into wine, then do we want to be poured out when we are full of that wine, or when we are near empty? Being poured out when your life is almost empty has very little effect, and we really want our life to count for as much as possible.

Word: "It's time to take off the filthy garments (death clothes) that you have been wearing while I have had you in the cave. Put on the new garments of the new anointing." Remember when Bathsheba and David's first son died? David got up from his prayers, he washed and put on new garments. Then he was ready to go on with what God was calling him to do. God is saying this to us. "Put on these new garments and go forward with what I am releasing you to do, or who I am freeing you to become."

An Example: We've known Mike and Jane (not their real names) for a short while, and Marlene and Jane have grown close. They both like to intercede, and they can stay on the phone for hours. Jane has been in leadership in a large ministry setting, and has been wounded. She has pulled into her shell, only coming out for a couple of close friends. Mike has been harder to get to know. He's not one to talk much about himself, but when he does, you can see that he is not happy with who he is. Mike is very intelligent and very analytical and has a harder time relating. Things that have been said about them have hamstrung them both. He has been in the cave for years; she is more of a new arrival.

Thankfully God is doing His thing. He is using us to take off the old garments and put on the new. God wants people to see themselves from His point of view and not the way others see them. Helping people see themselves as God does is great. Once they start catching on, the fun really begins. Getting them back in the race is most rewarding and it is filled with expectation of what God is going to do for them and for us.

PATIENCE AND LOVE

Another word for patience is long-suffering. Defined: Long means extended in distance and time, drawn-out, protracted. Suffer means to endure, to undergo, to allow, to undergo pain, punishment.

When you think of these words, who comes to your mind? Job? He lost his health, his family, his fortune. Or Joseph who spent two plus years in prison and 12 years in bondage, for something he didn't even do?

Do you think of Jesus who spent 40 days in the wilderness plus seven of the hardest days known to man? Or the children of Israel who wandered for 40 years in the wilderness?

How about Daniel who waited in the lion's den for his fate? Or Shadrach, Meshech, Abednego who were thrown into the fiery furnace?

How many long-suffering lessons has God had for you? I know for me it seems like too many. Don't quit when things start to get difficult. Push on, but be gentle. Remember God has called you to love His children, the ones He has brought into your life, back into wholeness as He did with you. David was faced with many challenges while God changed those hurt and wounded men into mighty warriors.

Another part of long-suffering I believe is shared in Matthew 5:43-48—love your enemy.

I think I am finally beginning to understand this command. I have not mastered it, but I am seeing there is a real purpose that I have not seen before. We've all read or heard this scripture: "*Iron sharpens iron, so one man sharpens another...*" (Proverbs 27:17). We can learn from our enemy. Notice that he is still an enemy but we can learn about ourselves from him. Why love him? Because loving your enemy is one of the refiners of our faith.

This is one sure way to find out whose purposes you have at heart. I can look back now and see how the Lord has used this principle in my life many times to bring about His plan of action for me. There were truths I would not receive any other way. Hurts, pain, and slander were brought on by my brothers and sisters in Christ (A better mirror to look into self cannot be bought). Nothing hurts more than being beat up by a Christian, but I've heard that the enemy always plants a little truth in every lie so it will hook you. I used to say that we could ignore it. Now the Lord is requiring me to look for that "little bit" of truth and see if it's something that God wants to remove out of my life. You know, like pride, or self-righteousness, or unforgiveness, or maybe ambition.

FAITHFULNESS

Faith: unquestioning belief that does not require proof or evidence. Keeping faith, full of faith. Bible faith: "*is the substance of things hoped for and the evidence of things not seen*"(Heb. 11:1 KJV).

God is faithful! One must look only at the Old Testament to see the unfaithfulness of man toward his God, and then easily see the converse truth. God repeatedly shows His faithfulness to us. Man breaks covenant with God; God corrects and forgives or sends a deliverer. Over and over He is faithful! Psalm 78 is a great example and paints a beautiful picture of His faithfulness compared to our human frailty.

The Word of God calls on us to be faithful to God. Why? *Not because of what he has done, but for* **who He is**.

What He has done for us only makes being faithful easier. In all things? Yes! The current catch phrase, "What would Jesus do?" might apply here. Jesus was faithful in all things even unto His death. Again, He is our model (2 Kings 23:25).

LEADERSHIP AND SERVANTHOOD

There must be leaders willing to break out of religious Christianity. A true leader must first be a good follower. God uses the Saul in our lives to get the Saul out of our lives.

Illustration: I sat under the teaching of Reverend Robert Pluimer for five years as he trained others and me for the ministry. "Pastor Butch," as he was known, was a great teacher, and I still hold on to much of those foundational teachings. Yet there were things that I struggled with in classes, things about which I didn't think I was on the same page with him. Some were presentational and some were doctrinal. When I mentioned this to his then-assistant pastor and my friend John Suitor, his response was interesting. He said that when I get my own church, I could do it my way. This has happened many times in my ministry now. God has used people and situations in our lives to bring about the changes that He wants in us. We see them as difficult, hard places to be in, but it's really only God's classroom. He must teach us how to *lead His way*!

This is the attitude you must have if you wish to honestly represent Jesus Christ.

Great people must be servants, servants of God, and servants of Christ, servants of all. Servanthood means that you are free to serve if you want to. It's an attitude that must be groomed, along with the correct motivation. Our example is, of course, Jesus. On His last free day with His disciples, what does He show (teach) them? Servanthood! (See John 13.)

Jesus, knowing who He is and what He is about to face, gives them their final lesson. He washes their feet. This is the lowest form of servanthood. Yet, this is what He models for us (this is also *a real flesh burner*).

You want me to do what? You want me to love my enemies and wash people's feet? How much of this do you think I can take, Lord?

Without Me, you (Duane, David, man, woman) *can do nothing!*

What Is God Speaking to Me?

_____

_____

_____

_____

_____

_____

_____

_____

_____

_____

_____

_____

_____

_____

_____

_____

_____

CHAPTER 17

WHAT'S NEXT?
RADICAL CHRISTIANITY!

I have been praying and asking the Lord this question: What's next? What do we do now? After coming on so strongly against the system and conservative, religious Christianity, what more do I say to you? I can't leave people here any more than I want to stay here.

This morning God spoke to me. In reality, I can see that He has been speaking this to us for a long time. Yesterday He used a person who I would not have guessed He would use to drop a nugget of pure gold in me. I have only met this man twice, and I called him to consult with me on designing a new website for the business I am working for. He had me set up a fake website so I could learn the software we are using, and I jokingly called it "Duane's Book." Chapter 1 was titled "I Hate Conservative Christianity." Well, this brought out of him a "Wow, what's that all about?" I gave him the premise of the book, namely that if you see Jesus on the Cross, what was conservative about that? His response was, "It was radical!" That was all that was said at the time. We had a lot to do.

> **Word:** This morning the Lord spoke using that same word—"radical." His word to me was "Radical Christianity cannot live in buildings made by human effort, it must live and can only be sustained by the power of God, in the temple of God."

When we set out to build a building, one of the first things we do is prepare the ground for the forms that we will use to contain the foundation. We pour the cement, frame the structures, and after that, we wall it in.

I think I am beginning to understand where the Lord wants to take the Church, and it is not forward. It is backward! Back to the days of those early disciples and how they followed Jesus' example of going from house to house. This is not kinships, home Bible studies, home groups, and home fellowships. This is Radical Christianity! Where did Jesus go? Matthew's house, Zacheus' house. He went to the homes of unbelievers, and they heard the truth. Not the same homes, He moved from place to place and house to house, and His followers did the same thing. Peter went to Cornelius' home even though it was against the law for him to do so. Philip went to the Ethiopians. They crossed lines that we have problems crossing today.

I believe that God was behind the scattering of the saints— what we call the great persecution! Even way back then they had already started to build walls around themselves. When we try to firmly structure what God is doing, He moves on. His power moves on, and we are left with only the remembrance of what it was like to be in His presence and how exciting it was. We cannot contain God, and when we try to hem Him in, to put Him in a box, He always, always gets out, and we are left with only an empty box—a pile of stones. We are His Temple who walk among His children.

Fellowship (gathering together in His name) is not meant for teaching only, although it is good to be taught. Fellowship is also meant to encourage one another to do good works in His name. The Body of Christ should be meeting to praise and worship God and to encourage His Body to take up our identity in Him and give it away to the world in power and authority. Pastors, mentors, mature believers, please share with people to be who the Holy Spirit is calling them to be and not to fill the need you have—do the things that Jesus did.

We, as the Body of Christ, have been so weakened that when Christians who have never been around the power of God or have never even seen Him in action see the power of the Holy Spirit, they think it is a hoax.

He will not do it our way. Do you want it easy? Clean, without a mess? Never gonna happen, saint! But, oh, how rewarding it can be when God works His healing or deliverance though you. Wow, what a rush!

Ask yourself these questions: Why did Christ come as a baby? Why did Jesus the Christ come as a child? Why a Son? Why did God choose this way? Why did Jesus live an ordinary life as a mere man for 30+ years?

Why?

So, you and I could *get it*! Get what? Get and understand what children of God are to be like! What our purpose is and how it should be walked out. What the power of God in us is all about. What life should look like—what it's for and how to use it. Why it was genetically given to us. Why it must be applied by using our faith. Hear me again!

Jesus is our model!

Remember this, there is room for Radical Christianity in every Christian church and in every Christian denomination. Unlike conservative and religious Christianity, radical Christianity has no bounds because you are not listening to man, but to God. Tune your heart to His, and let Him decide where He wants to take you. Hold on tight, because I guarantee the ride is going to be excitingly great. Sometimes you'll want to get off and rest awhile, but hang in there. If you are faithful with what He wants you to do, lives will be changed and the Kingdom of God will be built up. In the midst of this, you may be asked to leave the church you attend or serve at. But never fear; they can't make you leave the Body of Christ Jesus.

BE PREPARED

We were visiting a local church on New Year's Eve one year, and as I was worshiping I saw a very clear picture of spiritual warfare. I had my hands raised over my head and there was darkness all around. My hands were together and my arms were raised straight up, as in a swimming stroke. As I began to bring my arms down to my sides, light came and filled the place where my hands had been. The more I brought them down the more light filled that space. When I reached the halfway point, with my arms straight out to my sides, it became more difficult to move them. I seemed to know that this was the earth, ground level, and then

I pressed on, harder, firmer, and now I knew that I was forcing the darkness back into hell.

The picture was of dispelling darkness with worship. Swimming through darkness and bringing the light as I went. I saw myself swimming through darkness and leaving a trail of light behind me.

Not only is worship a wonderful time of bringing glory to God, but satan hates worship because we have joined our spirit to the Spirit of God and we, together, are pushing back the gates of hell. Come forth, Lord! Let your Kingdom break forth in us, your body. Your Kingdom come; your will be done. Your rule in us, your rule through us, on earth as it is in Heaven.

Lord, help us to recognize the rule of your Kingdom in our lives.

When we understand whose Kingdom this is, who we really belong to, who bought us, and what a great price was paid so we could be a part of Your kingdom, free from the kingdom of darkness and its authority, and free to live in the kingdom of light, then we, as a people of God, will truly be free.

This story has always helped me understand the concept of living in God's Kingdom. Go back with me to the days of kings and castles and knights with their armor and the powerful horses they rode on.

I see a land of peasants and farmers and their village. In the center of this village, a post stands. It's just a large wooden post in the ground, called a post because that is where important notices are "posted." If the king who rules this part of the country has any news, rules, or taxes, he has them "posted" here.

Now see with me that on a quiet morning the people in the village, which lies just below the castle, are beginning to awake.

They hear the large drawbridge opening, and soon they hear the hooves of the horses galloping across the drawbridge which spans the moat. The knights ride from the castle down into the center of the village and then right up to the post, bringing their horses to a sudden halt. Dust flies in a cloud. I can see the nostrils flare and the hoofs pawing the ground. One of the knights unscrolls a parchment notice while another draws his sword and with the butt end of his gleaming sword, he nails the parchment to the post. Then just like they arrived, they ride off, back to the castle, across the moat and disappear inside (old style e-mail). As they leave, all the people come out to read the new set of rules that have just been posted. On it they read what the cost is going to be for living under the protection of the king.

This scene has been played out in many of the old movies, but I see it as a picture of what God has done for us. First He posted His Word for us to read, then He posted the ten rules, then He posted Himself.

If you and I choose to live in His Kingdom, then we must live by what is posted. Of course, if you should choose not to live by these, there is another set you will live by. It lists all the consequences for those who choose to ignore His set.

I know, you don't like the word *rules*. However, we are not forced to live by them. Only if we want to take full advantage of His protection, and all that His Word has to say is available to those who choose to live by His Word for us. I don't know about you, but I want it all.

If you choose to, pray this prayer with me, "Lord, I give You permission to have Your way in me. Help me, Lord, to become all that You have designed me for. Do whatever it takes in me to bring me to that place." (Take my word that this is a dangerous prayer if you don't mean it.)

BREAKING OUT

From the beginning, God has shown us that the dispersion of seed is the key to conception and life. From what we call "nature," which I believe has been carved out from God's nature, we see this truth; and then from the creation, we see it even more clearly. The principle is that if you have something and you want it to be reproduced, you must plant it. When we speak what we really believe, we are planting seeds.

As I close this book, I know that some of you will be upset with some of what I have written. I hope so. Not that I look forward to people disagreeing with me, but my hope is that this book has made you think beyond the cave, think without being stuck, think without being unteachable. I want you to know, to understand, and to be filled with passion for what you believe. It's important that we don't just say what others say and just believe what others have told us is correct.

If you are fervent in your views, filled with passion for what you believe, then you will speak out, and when you do, you will be planting seeds. My prayer is that the seeds I have spoken in this book, those which reflect the truth of God, will be planted and those which reflect my flesh, or any rebellion, God will not germinate.

Will you join me in that prayer for yourselves? I believe that we, you and I, do not want anything to grow that is not of God.

I have been accused of "pushing the envelope." Pushing the envelope—operating outside the prescribed design specifications—contains more risk, yet it can be much more rewarding. You are on the cutting edge of technology, the edge of understanding, seeing what was thought to be impossible unfold before your very eyes.

Pushing the envelope is where Christianity began and where I personally believe that it is supposed to operate. God continues to reveal more of Himself and His plan and more of who we were created to be in Him. Do we deny this or do we go with it? I want to be caught living on the edge of Christianity. Never going outside boundaries set by the Word of God but always willing to obey the voice of God no matter how it may stretch me and my views. We need to escape any box that people try to stuff us into. Let's look for a fresh paradigm to live in and to see God through. Scriptures tell us that He is bigger than anything we can imagine. May God truly bless us with a fresh view of our identity in Him.

A WORD FROM THE SPIRIT

The Lord is approaching. Do you see Him there? Run, run to draw near, catch hold of Him as He slows, He looks, He calls. Are you there?

Don't miss what He brings as He passes near; reach out, He waits, He longs for you. He longs to touch you, to hold you, to kiss you, to embrace you. Don't miss it; don't miss out. He's so close. Look, He's calling for you. So sweet the sound, so sweet the voice, He leaves me breathless waiting for another touch.

WHO WILL GO?

"I will," says the Word of God! How will you go? "As one of them, so they can see a model of righteousness! They need a pattern—One with skin and bones. One born of a virgin and who comes from the ground up. They need a Perfect Sacrifice."

"*...receive with meekness the engrafted word, which is able to save your souls*" (James 1:21 KJV)—the Word implanted in you.

What Is God Speaking to Me?

_____

_____

_____

_____

_____

_____

_____

_____

_____

_____

_____

_____

_____

_____

_____

_____

_____

_____

_____

_____

_____

Additional copies of this book and other
book titles from DESTINY IMAGE are
available at your local bookstore.

Call toll free: 1-800-722-6774.

Send a request for a catalog to:

Destiny Image® Publishers, Inc.

P.O. Box 310
Shippensburg, PA 17257-0310

*"Speaking to the Purposes of God for this
Generation and for the Generations to Come."*

For a complete list of our titles,
visit us at www.destinyimage.com